KAREEM MOODY

with Anitra Budd

raise them up:

the real deal on
reaching unreachable
kids

Search
INSTITUTE

Raise Them Up:
The Real Deal on Reaching
Unreachable Kids
Kareem Moody with Anitra Budd

Printed on acid-free paper in the
United States of America.

Search Institute
615 First Avenue Northeast
Suite 125
Minneapolis, MN 55413
www.search-institute.org
612-376-8955
800-888-7828

Credits
Editor: Anitra Budd
Book Design: Jeenee Lee
Production Coordinator:
Mary Ellen Buscher

Library of Congress
Cataloging-in-Publication Data

Moody, Kareem.
    Raise them up : the real deal
    on reaching unreachable kids /
    by Kareem Moody with
    Anitra Budd.
        p. cm.
    ISBN-13: 978-1-57482-866-5
    (pbk. : alk. paper)
    ISBN-10: 1-57482-866-5
    (pbk. : alk. paper)

    1. Problem children—
       United States
    2. Adolescent psychology—
       United States.
    3. Youth development—
       United States.
    4. Social work with youth—
       United States.
    5. Mentoring—United States.
    6. Youth—Counseling of—
       United States.
    I. Budd, Anitra.
    II. Title.

This book is dedicated to the hundreds of young people I've worked with over the years who've allowed me to be a part of their lives; all the staff and students from the Clark County Boys and Girls Club, the Step Up Support Center, and Positive Atmosphere Reaches Kids (P.A.R.K.); and the many young people I've run across on America's playgrounds, basketball courts, and street corners.

contents

acknowledgments

SPECIAL thanks to God for giving me the focus and energy to love kids, even when I thought I should be doing something more prestigious. Thanks to my wife, Rona, who encouraged me while I wrote the first draft, supported me when I didn't feel like working on it, and loved me every step of the way even when I didn't practice what I preached. I also want to thank "them Moody boys," who unselfishly gave up their dad/uncle so he could help other kids get the good things they have. Thanks to my sisters, who've always loved what I was when others just loved what they thought I was, and to my niece and sister-in-law for blossoming as they have. I also offer a special thank-you to Keith and Melanie Jackson for allowing me to nurture their vision.

I'd like to give a special acknowledgment to my Oakwood bayou, cotton-and-soybean-field family, who instilled in me a respect for my family legacy. Thanks as well to my grandparents and great-grandparents for their many sacrifices and the values they taught me. To the streets of Houston, Texas; Dumas, Arkansas; and Chicago, Illinois—thanks for not taking me under even when I was begging to go. A special thanks to my old man (may he rest in peace) for giving me what he could from what he had.

Most of all, I want to thank my momma (Ma) for the way she taught me to love by example, for her patience and her unyielding belief in the human spirit, and for always making me feel like the king of the hill.

THE YEARS I spent as a professional football player taught me many important lessons, one of which was discipline. Most of the coaches I've known, from Little League right up to the NFL, were a lot like drill sergeants. If you were late, the coach would make you run. If you made too many mistakes, the coach would make you run. If you were disobedient, the coach would make you run. The answer for almost every infraction was to make players run until their tongues fell out! Now that I'm in my 40s, I've learned to appreciate not only those coaches, but the teachers, administrators, and youth workers I've worked with who also believe in consistent and appropriate correction for youth.

For many adults, however, it can be hard to know when and how to correct young people, particularly those young people who seem "unreachable." Today's youth are very different from those in previous generations. They might not respond to the same level of authority or discipline you did when you were young. The phrases parents and teachers drilled into our heads, things like "yes sir," "thank you," "please," and "you're welcome," might not come as easily to their lips. And sadly, my work with young people has forced me to face the reality that far too many of our kids are being raised in unstable, dysfunctional environments. These factors and many others can make young people seem hard to connect to at times. But instead of just giving up on them, we must keep asking ourselves the question, "How can I reach out to 'unreachable' youth?"

Kareem Moody is remarkably talented when it comes to providing answers to that question. I personally believe that God has blessed him with special insight into the minds of hard-to-reach teens. I've worked with Kareem for the last eight years, and every time a situation arises with one of the young people at our youth center, he always corrects it by teaching. A large part of his brilliance is built on his passion for raising tomorrow's leaders, a passion that comes from a tough upbringing in the School of Hard Knocks. The way Kareem gracefully maneuvers through the tough problems kids face doesn't come from a Ph.D.—it's largely due to the fact that he has a B.H. (Big Heart).

I've had some great teammates in my day. The men I've played with, whether on the Miami Dolphins, the Philadelphia Eagles, or the Green Bay Packers, were incredible athletes and colleagues. But in the fight to save our nation's youth, I'm glad it's Kareem Moody who is on my team. I hope his wisdom in reaching the unreachable will help you the way it has helped the many teens whose lives he's already touched.

KEITH JACKSON
Founder
Positive Atmosphere Reaches Kids (P.A.R.K.)
www.positivekids.org

It is far easier to build strong children than to repair broken adults. [FREDERICK DOUGLASS]

MY NAME

is Kareem Moody. I'm the father of two wonderful boys, and as I write this I work at Positive Atmosphere Reaches Kids (P.A.R.K.), an after-school youth program that helps teens who are in danger of dropping out of school. But long before I ever worked with young people, I was one of *those* kids. You know, the kind of kid you have trouble reaching. The one with a chip on his shoulder who you hope your kid doesn't meet. The one you hate to see walking into your youth center. Yes, that was me—the kid most people said wouldn't amount to anything.

Raise Them Up is about how you could've dealt with me when I was *that* kid. It was inspired by the many frustrated parents and youth workers I meet in the course of my work who are searching for ways to reach their "unreachable" kids. They're at their wit's end and feel they've tried just about every idea out there for dealing with hard-to-reach kids. Many of you reading this book feel exactly the same way. You've made numerous attempts, explored dozens of options, and still find yourself on the outside looking in on the world of teens in high-risk situations. Perhaps you're becoming more and more confused as you and your teenage son or daughter grow further apart, and have found yourself wondering if you have the strength to make it through yet another crisis or fight. Maybe you're a youth worker who began a career with so much hope, and now wake up every morning facing your workday with dread and fatigue. Don't be ashamed; many adults faced with the realities of supporting hard-to-reach young people question their endurance. Many, if not most, also wish there was a place they could go for a quick fix for their problem. This book won't give you any ready-made solutions; every child and every situation is different. But it will help spark your creativity and, more importantly, give you a renewed sense of purpose and energy.

Some of the stories in this book are tough to read. Trust me, they were hard to live through, too. They reveal the tragic lives—and, in some cases, deaths—of real young people. I don't sugarcoat these stories because I think they can teach valuable lessons to people who are raising and working with "difficult" youth.

ARE YOU A DOCTOR?

I don't have a master's, a Ph.D., or any other advanced degree to speak of. I'm just a regular guy who happens to be passionate about working with young people. Over the years I've learned some things about them, and have decided to share what I know with anyone who sees or knows children they just don't understand. While I don't claim to have all the answers, this book will give you some useful suggestions for building positive relationships with young people.

My advice is based in something called the Developmental Assets. The name might sound intimidating, but all it means is "the good things all kids need to grow up healthy and happy." The Developmental Assets were developed by Search Institute, a nonprofit organization in Minneapolis, Minnesota, that is committed to researching healthy development in children and adolescents. Researchers have discovered over the years that the more of these positive experiences, qualities, and relationships (or "assets") that young people have, the better. Best of all, when you look at young people through the lens of Developmental Assets, your focus is on all the positive opportunities in their lives instead of just the risks and mistakes. This is a win-win approach—not only are young people likely to feel more hopeful about themselves and their futures, but you'll feel more optimistic about their chances as well.

MORE ABOUT DEVELOPMENTAL ASSETS

The Developmental Assets framework was first introduced in 1990. At that time, Search Institute identified and measured 30 Developmental Assets.

Search Institute continued to review the research and

conduct studies, surveying more than 350,000 students in grades 6 through 12 between 1990 and 1995. The surveys revealed the Developmental Assets they experienced, the risks they took, the obstacles they had to overcome, and the ways they thrived. The institute also conducted numerous informal discussions and focus groups. As a result of these ongoing research activities, in 1996 the Developmental Assets framework was revised into its current form, a model of 40 Developmental Assets for adolescents.

What follows here is Search Institute's list of 40 Developmental Assets for Adolescents (ages 12 –18). The institute continues its long-term research efforts to refine, measure, and test the asset frameworks for children of all ages. For free, downloadable asset lists in different languages (French and Spanish) and for different age groups, please visit www.search-institute.org/assets.

40 Developmental Assets for Adolescents
(Ages 12–18)

Search Institute has identified the following building blocks of healthy development that help young people grow up healthy, caring, and responsible.

External assets

SUPPORT
1. *Family support*—Family life provides high levels of love and support.
2. *Positive family communication*—Young person and her or his parent(s) communicate positively, and young person is willing to seek advice and counsel from parents.

3. *Other adult relationships*—Young person receives support from three or more nonparent adults.
4. *Caring neighborhood*—Young person experiences caring neighbors.
5. *Caring school climate*—School provides a caring, encouraging environment.
6. *Parent involvement in schooling*—Parent(s) are actively involved in helping young person succeed in school.

EMPOWERMENT

7. *Community values youth*—Young person perceives that adults in the community value youth.
8. *Youth as resources*—Young people are given useful roles in the community.
9. *Service to others*—Young person serves in the community one hour or more per week.
10. *Safety*—Young person feels safe at home, school, and in the neighborhood.

BOUNDARIES AND EXPECTATIONS

11. *Family boundaries*—Family has clear rules and consequences and monitors the young person's whereabouts.
12. *School boundaries*—School provides clear rules and consequences.
13. *Neighborhood boundaries*—Neighbors take responsibility for monitoring young people's behavior.
14. *Adult role models*—Parent(s) and other adults model positive, responsible behavior.
15. *Positive peer influence*—Young person's best friends model responsible behavior.
16. *High expectations*—Both parent(s) and teachers encourage the young person to do well.

17. *Creative activities*—Young person spends three or more hours per week in lessons or practice in music, theater, or other arts.

18. *Youth programs*—Young person spends three or more hours per week in sports, clubs, or organizations at school and/or in the community.

19. *Religious community*—Young person spends one or more hours per week in activities in a religious institution.

20. *Time at home*—Young person is out with friends "with nothing special to do" two or fewer nights per week.

Internal assets

COMMITMENT TO LEARNING

21. *Achievement motivation*—Young person is motivated to do well in school.

22. *School engagement*—Young person is actively engaged in learning.

23. *Homework*—Young person reports doing at least one hour of homework every school day.

24. *Bonding to school*—Young person cares about her or his school.

25. *Reading for pleasure*—Young person reads for pleasure three or more hours per week.

POSITIVE VALUES

26. *Caring*—Young person places high value on helping other people.

27. *Equality and social justice*—Young person places high value on promoting equality and reducing hunger and poverty.

28. *Integrity*—Young person acts on convictions and stands up for her or his beliefs.

29. *Honesty*—Young person "tells the truth even when it is not easy."

30. *Responsibility*—Young person accepts and takes personal responsibility.

31. *Restraint*—Young person believes it is important not to be sexually active or to use alcohol or other drugs.

SOCIAL COMPETENCIES

32. *Planning and decision making*—Young person knows how to plan ahead and make choices.

33. *Interpersonal competence*—Young person has empathy, sensitivity, and friendship skills.

34. *Cultural competence*—Young person has knowledge of and comfort with people of different cultural/racial/ethnic backgrounds.

35. *Resistance skills*—Young person can resist negative peer pressure and dangerous situations.

36. *Peaceful conflict resolution*—Young person seeks to resolve conflict nonviolently.

POSITIVE IDENTITY

37. *Personal power*—Young person feels he or she has control over "things that happen to me."

38. *Self-esteem*—Young person reports having a high self-esteem.

39. *Sense of purpose*—Young person reports that "my life has a purpose."

40. *Positive view of personal future*—Young person is optimistic about her or his personal future.

The Developmental Assets are spread across eight broad areas of human development. The first four asset categories focus on external structures, relationships, and activities that create a positive environment for young people:

SUPPORT
Young people need to be surrounded by people who love, care for, appreciate, and accept them. They need to know that they belong and that they are not alone.

EMPOWERMENT
Young people need to feel valued and valuable. This happens when youth feel safe, when they believe they are liked and respected, and when they contribute to their families and communities.

BOUNDARIES AND EXPECTATIONS
Young people need the positive influence of peers and adults who encourage them to be and do their best. Youth also need clear rules about appropriate behavior and consistent, reasonable consequences for breaking those rules.

CONSTRUCTIVE USE OF TIME
Young people need opportunities—outside of school—to learn and develop new skills and interests, and to spend enjoyable time interacting with other youth and adults.

The next four categories reflect internal values, skills, and beliefs young people also need to develop to fully engage with and function in the world around them:

COMMITMENT TO LEARNING
Young people need a variety of learning experiences,

including the desire for academic success, a sense of the lasting importance of learning, and a belief in their own abilities.

POSITIVE VALUES
Young people need to develop strong guiding values or principles, including caring about others, having high standards for personal character, and believing in protecting their own well-being.

SOCIAL COMPETENCIES
Young people need to develop the skills to interact effectively with others, to make difficult decisions and choices, and to cope with new situations.

POSITIVE IDENTITY
Young people need to believe in their own self-worth, to feel they have control over the things that happen to them, and to have a sense of purpose in life as well as a positive view of the future.

HOW CAN THIS BOOK HELP ME?

Now that you've learned a little about Developmental Assets, you might be wondering how you can use the framework to help young people. The good news is that the assets are powerful and everyone can build them (when you intentionally help youth develop these strengths, you're *building assets*). Search Institute's research shows that the more assets young people have, the more likely they are to make positive choices in life and to avoid risky activities like sex, violence, and substance abuse. The challenge for all of us is that most young people aren't experiencing enough of the assets.

I've included stories in this book that say something about the impact asset building had on various young people I've known (myself included), whether they benefited from the experience or could have used more positive help than I gave at the time. These reflections will give you ideas about how you can incorporate assets into your relationships with youth, especially the hard-to-reach ones. Although you can and should adjust the lessons in these stories to your own situation, "Raise Them Up" tips are included at the end of each story to give specific, positive suggestions about reaching out to teens. There are also six bonus tips at the end of the book that will arm you with some extra advice. Next to each tip you'll see one of the eight asset-category icons (for example, a light bulb for Commitment to Learning, a compass for Positive Values) to let you know which category the tip supports.

THE SKY'S THE LIMIT

I sincerely hope *Raise Them Up* offers a fresh start to you and the young people you care about. No matter what's happened up to this moment, there's always a new opportunity to help hard-to-reach youth grow into happy, confident, and healthy adults. Keep your expectations and your attitudes high, and see just how much you can accomplish together. Good luck to both you and the young people in your life as you work on building positive relationships.

fractured friendship

The moment I saw the pack of shouting teens
outside my window one evening at work, I knew
I had a learning opportunity in front of me.

Two girls were arguing loudly in the center of the crowd.
They were at each other's throats and obviously upset. Despite
the high level of tension, neither had physically touched the
other yet, and as I learned when I was a kid, if two people are
shouting face-to-face and nobody throws a punch, those
people don't really want to fight. This is especially true if the
two are friends.

Friendships carry a lot of weight, and young people want
to keep their friends. Unfortunately what typically happens is

that friends think it's more important to "save face" than make up after an argument. To young people, it seems as if their entire world rests on their reputation. They think if they leave a fight looking scared or weak, they're more likely to get attacked by others who witness the altercation, or hear about it through the grapevine. In this instance, neither girl was about to let that happen by backing down first.

The gathering crowd clearly wanted to see a fight. Luckily, another student who happened to be friends with both girls stepped in and broke it up. By the time the girls were escorted by a staff member to my office, they were very distraught. Apparently, one girl was spreading lies about the other. They'd been having this problem for some time, and today it had come to a head.

Having worked with young people over the years, I know one fact forever rings true: Kids are going to have disagreements, even with their close friends. Maybe they'll be interested in the same boy or girl, or they'll claim, "He said this," or "She said that." Having arguments is a part of being human.

What's important is how adults—program directors, youth workers, parents, coaches, teachers, social workers, truant officers, whoever you are—help kids learn to deal with these conflicts. We adults can't fight their battles and steer them away from all disagreements. Instead, we can try to help them work *through* disagreements, so they're equipped to deal with future disputes.

I've found that if you can give young people a reasonable solution for resolving a conflict, most times they'll accept it—provided you're offering an approach that focuses on their strengths. And if you can convince them to stop worrying about saving face, most young people will realize the conflict they had wasn't that serious in the first place. It's the overwhelming concern about reputation that can push disagreements past the point of no return.

In my situation, the first step had already been taken—getting the conflict confined to as small a group as possible. Now, in my office, it was just the three of us: two former best friends and one concerned program director. How was I going to get them talking? I knew these girls had been the best of friends at one point, which meant they had a lot of shared memories. I also knew they had enough respect for me to sit and talk, or to at least give it a try. When you are helping young people resolve conflicts, it's an enormous help to have their respect from the beginning of your relationship, prior to any issues coming up.

I had the girls sit in hardback chairs facing one another, knees touching. By having young people sit face-to-face, you allow them to confront the situation head-on, literally and figuratively, and to voice their frustrations in a calm setting. This setup gives them a chance to listen to each other and decide if they really have a serious problem in the first place. Often young people will get into an altercation without knowing what they're upset about, or knowing if they're really upset at all.

It's the overwhelming concern about reputation that can push disagreements past the point of no return.

When mediating a fight, I like to begin with a little small talk. My tone—one of "a mistake has been made and we're all here to correct it"—never changes. I also try to start off with some shocking statement the kids wouldn't expect me to say. This usually startles them so much they forget they're upset, and I'll go on in this way until they figure out what I'm up to. In this case, I purposely asked the girls if they were fighting over a boy I knew neither liked. I wondered aloud what embarrassing rumors would start circulating, all because of their battle over a guy. I continued on, casually talking about how this must look to the other students, and asking if the winner of their fight would get the boy as her prize.

Naturally, the girls hurried to correct my "mistake." They decided to fill me in on what really happened, both raising their voices over the other in their rush to be heard. I said, "Let the person who started it go first." Both stopped abruptly, only to start up more loudly than before, trying to pass the blame.

Seeing we were getting nowhere fast, I chose one girl and asked her to tell me her side of the story, telling the other that if she didn't disrupt the story she'd get to talk without interruption later. I told them both to listen and take notes while the other talked, so the listener could respond when it was her turn to speak. This is an important part of the mediation process, because it requires each to hear the other's perspective.

By starting off the discussion this way, I helped the girls feel more open to resolving their problem peacefully. Then, I started looking for ways to involve them in the process more directly. Gradually, throughout the conversation, I gave them chances to start taking their fair share of the blame, pausing or pointing out the places where they might have done something offensive or hurtful. On their own, they began to recognize how they might've acted unfairly, or could've handled things differently. I prodded each to sympathize with the other, saying, "Do you think she meant to hurt you?" or "I bet she wishes she could take that back." By apologizing for them both, I was making it easier for them to eventually take the lead and start apologizing for themselves.

I told them how important it was to cherish friends. I talked about what cool friends they'd been; when they were together, they spread fun and laughter wherever they went. I reminded them of the good and bad times they'd shared, and that the people they cared about might not be around forever. Both could name past friends who were once in our center's program but had moved away or just stopped attending altogether.

At this point the girls were no longer snarling at each other, and instead were laughing along with me as I continued to talk about their happy times. They were far removed from the fight, and nearing the "alright point"—the moment when it feels safe to apologize. Now it was just a matter of helping the girls close the deal by giving them a final chance to save face with their friend, and hopefully their peers as well.

I told them each to write a poem about the other, right there in my office. Even though I didn't ask them to share the poems or read them aloud, when they were finished they immediately exchanged papers and read the poems to each other. This was especially touching because both girls did this of their own accord, and it gave each a chance to see what her friend was feeling.

Since I'd asked them to write the poems on the spot and hadn't given them any time for revision, the poems were fairly simple. The girls were so embarrassed by their "corny" rhymes that they now had a joint interest again—keeping those poems secret from their friends! But even though they didn't produce masterpieces, they were able to walk away with something they could laugh about—and laughter's second only to hugs in its ability to mend friendships. Pretty soon all three of us were cracking up like old friends—which is exactly what the two girls had become again.

☺ Writing can be a great aid to helping young people solve conflicts, whether you ask them to write down their thoughts before speaking, to write down and repeat what they believe the other person is saying, or to write down ideas on how to keep the peace after the conflict is resolved.

☺ When you are mediating an argument between young people, refrain from playing favorites by letting one person talk more than another, or making comments like, "Just apologize to her, it's clear it was your fault." As much as possible, allow the young people to work toward a solution with minimal input from you.

☺ Sometimes young people can say things on an impulse that they don't mean, especially in the heat of an argument. Allow them to take breaks from a discussion if tensions are running high, or make a rule that they have to take at least 30 minutes to calm down before beginning to resolve a conflict.

gangsta rapper

One spring day, a staff member rushed two
P.A.R.K. program participants into my office,
informing me that the school bus driver had
caught the boys fighting on the bus. I was very
embarrassed for the program, the boys, and
myself. Although many young people come to
P.A.R.K. with reputations for bad behavior,
most participants work hard to overcome their
past problems. I was sorry the bus driver had
seen this sort of behavior from our kids.

When the three of us were alone, I offered the two boys a seat. Ron, the older of the pair, was a short, stocky kid who was pretty serious about becoming a rap artist. At the time he had a group that performed at parties and other places around town. He'd even performed at P.A.R.K. a couple of times, where both staff and students had praised his talent. The other boy, Jake, was tall and slender. I was aware from years of knowing both boys that Jake didn't like Ron much, musical talent or not.

During the time Ron had been at P.A.R.K., I'd noticed how much he wanted the kind of positive attention he'd gotten at those rap performances. Unfortunately, when he wasn't sure how to get good attention, he resorted to purposely annoying people to get any kind of response. This habit had made him pretty unpopular with the other students and, I suspected, provoked the fight on the bus. But at that time I withheld judgment and simply asked Ron to tell me what happened, from his perspective.

He explained that he'd been memorizing some new material and on this particular day, he just happened to be reciting the lyrics on the bus. Jake jumped in to tell me that one of the songs had some very vulgar language and was particularly insulting to women. He went on to say that one young lady grew so tired of the offensive rhymes that she offered five dollars to anyone who could shut Ron up. Jake happily accepted the job and carried it out by hitting Ron in the face. Ron didn't retaliate because by then all of the other young people on the bus were firmly on Jake's side. Luckily the bus driver intervened before the situation got any worse.

After finishing their separate versions of the stories, the two boys sat in front of me with hangdog expressions, waiting expectantly for the punishments they knew were coming. First,

I explained to Jake that he had no right to put his hands on another person. As noble as his intentions might've been, he was wrong for the way he'd handled the situation. Knowing he didn't like to write, I instructed him to spend the rest of the afternoon composing a three-page paper on bullying. I also told him to apologize to Ron in front of all the program members and staff the next morning, and to miss his recreation time for a couple of days. He admitted that he was wrong for hitting Ron, and that he felt he'd gotten off easy since fighting is a serious offense at P.A.R.K. He left quickly.

I turned my attention to Ron. I realized his role in the fight called for a special response, one uniquely geared toward his attention-seeking tendencies. My gut told me that if I didn't take strong measures to help him realize the effects his actions had on other people, he might someday end up in an altercation with much more drastic consequences than a punch to the face. Coming up with an idea on the spot, I first admitted how sorry I was about what had happened to him. I told him emphatically that I supported his right to say whatever he wanted, and that if he wanted to be a gangsta rapper he should go right ahead. In fact, to his surprise, I asked to hear the lyrics myself.

He was of course self-conscious about letting me, an adult authority figure, hear them, but I kept pressing the issue. He hesitantly began to rap. I told him to use all the profanity he'd been using earlier. I even asked him to get into character and bounce to the beat as I pounded on my desk.

Once he became more relaxed, I began calling in other staff members to listen. To Ron's surprise, I invited every available female staff person he knew—all women he respected very much. Before long the room was filled with lots of eyes, all watching as I urged him to sing louder. I shouted to him over the lyrics that gangsta rappers have to block out the crowd, that they can't let their feelings get in the way, that in his career, he'd have to face all sorts of people who'd be offended by his music—but he couldn't let that stop him.

As he continued to recite the obscenities, I loudly repeated them until finally, as he stared into all those disappointed faces, he began to cry. He'd learned the lesson, and I asked everyone to leave so the two of us could talk.

I knew Ron was having some trouble at home, and was most likely using music as a way to vent his frustration and earn the attention he wanted so badly. I also understood that he was just reciting the lyrics the way he'd heard them, and hadn't added in his own personality, talent, or imagination. I challenged him to be more creative, to really think about what *he* wanted to say instead of just mouthing someone else's words. To give him an incentive, I said he could be the headliner for our next talent show if he could show me the range and diversity in his music.

One of the powerful outcomes of this incident was learning how everyday conflicts, like a school bus fight, can grow from very complex roots. The situation wasn't just about a slap in the face; it pitted an individual youth's freedom of expression against his moral responsibility to the people he

I challenged him to be more creative, to really think about what *he* wanted to say instead of just mouthing someone else's words.

admired. As I told him, even though he had the right to rap in any way he wanted, he'd learned that he had to take other people's feelings into account. Having people in his life he respected, and whose respect he wanted, made the issue of free speech much more complicated.

Ron was humbled by the experience, and a few months later, when we were able to look back on it and laugh, he said it was one of the worst moments in his musical career. He went on to graduate from P.A.R.K. without any further incidents, and with a newfound respect for the power of words. When I saw him recently, he was hoping to become a mainstream poet and about to release his first rap album—which he quickly and proudly pointed out was completely free of profanity.

RAISE THEM UP:

Your messages will have more power if they are relevant to the personal experiences of the young people in your care. For instance, in this situation you might say, "Ron, how would you feel if someone was shouting these lyrics around your mother or sister?"

It's common for young people to act one way around friends, another way around their families, yet another way around teachers, and so on. When you notice young people expressing the same values and opinions around a variety of people, make sure to compliment them on their integrity and honesty.

Remember to keep your discussions with young people focused on the real issues at hand. For example, if teens are playing loud music in an area where people are trying to study, concentrate your comments on being respectful of others rather than criticizing their musical taste.

i hate school

One morning I came in to work and the
receptionist gave me a message: a man named
Tony had called and said he'd stop by to see
me later that day. He'd told her I would know
who he was, but I honestly couldn't say I did.
Puzzled, I went up to my office, set the message
aside, and sat down to work.

I spent most of the day playing the name over and
over in my head, trying to jog my memory. That afternoon my
musing was interrupted when a tall, lanky man with a deep
voice walked into my office and said, "Hello." When I looked

up, he broke into a big smile and said, "I'm done." I immediately recognized him: it was Tony, a young man who'd just finished four years at my alma mater. When he'd started college I'd told him I would have a job for him after graduation, and he'd apparently remembered that conversation. Although Tony would eventually take another job instead of the one I offered, his visit prompted me to reflect on the connections between school and lifelong education.

Years before, I was Tony's mentor while I was working as the assistant director of the Clark County Boys and Girls Club. The club is in Arkadelphia, a rural southwest Arkansas college town of about 11,000. Tony, a 7th grader, was one of the neighborhood kids who frequented the program. At that time I wouldn't have picked him as a favorite to even go to college, much less graduate. His home situation wasn't the best, he lived in the low-income part of town, and he was often hungry when he made it to the center, as were most of his buddies. Many of his friends had also been petty thieves, shoplifting regularly from a nearby convenience store.

The two of us reminisced about some of the other kids who were in the program with him. A few had gone to college, some were working at local factories, and, yes, a number were in or had gone to prison. We chatted about one young man in particular who'd gotten in a lot of trouble as a kid. Although he was very intelligent, he'd fallen two years behind in school. After working hard to catch up, he was in graduate school and working as a teacher in a local high school.

Thinking of all the different choices those other young people had made prompted me to ask Tony what made him choose *his* particular path. When he replied, "I enjoyed learning," it was refreshing to hear. He'd realized early on that he didn't have to make the same self-destructive decisions some of his friends had made, and that learning new things was the key to becoming the man he wanted to be. Although many of his friends hadn't liked school, his exposure to the different people and activities at the club had given him a broader outlook on the world and its possibilities.

I've discovered over the years that when children decide they hate school, they may soon begin to reject *all* kinds of learning. With this outlook on education, many young people go through years of school, and possibly life, without ever being truly affected by something in a way that changes their thinking.

There are a number of reasons kids dislike school— "boring" subjects, bullies, grades, rules, and, sometimes, tragic acts of violence. Think about it: Are there many adults who would want to go through junior high school again? In addition, kids often think schools aren't really built for them. Instead, they believe schools are simply a way for parents, teachers, politicians, and other adults to keep kids busy.

There is something adults can do to change this attitude: instead of forcing a particular school routine *on* kids, work to create a love of learning *in* kids. That love will keep them interested in school, and education in general, on their own. Have a talk with the children you care about and find out what gets them excited. Encourage them to share as much about the activities they love as possible. Make those activities the center of your focus, and show them how education can make their passions even more exciting, and help them achieve their

Kids often think schools aren't really built for them. Instead, they believe schools are simply a way for parents, teachers, politicians, and other adults to keep kids busy.

goals. For example, many of the inner-city boys I've worked with are interested in the entertainment industry. Learning math, reading, and time management skills in school will help these young men become the successful and creative professionals they aspire to be.

For those children who claim they don't have any special interests or talents, keep asking them questions. Try starting with, "What did you do today?" or "Who did you talk to in school?" These questions might bring up answers that seem like dead ends, such as "I hung out with my friends," or "I just played video games," but following up on these responses with questions like, "What is the video game about? What do you have to do to get a high score?" can lead to much deeper information about a young person's passions. For example, maybe a really talkative child would excel at being a news reporter, or a teen who's constantly taking pictures on a cameraphone might enjoy a photography class. However small the opening is, keep showing an interest. It's your genuine curiosity that allows young people to open up and reveal their unique abilities.

Many young people already have a passion (or something they would enjoy learning) burning inside them. They're not only looking for ways to share these passions, but also longing to prove to the world that they're special. It's frustrating to them when they're placed in environments that force-feed them information without acknowledging their different interests, goals, and learning styles. Sadly, some schools have a reputation for being just that kind of place.

It's your genuine curiosity that allows young people to open up and reveal their unique abilities.

So, when a kid says to you, "I hate school," know that what he's really saying is, "My school and I don't have anything in common," or "My school won't let me be me." By nurturing their dreams, you can create a fertile ground of excitement and curiosity in children. Teachers and parents can then plant the seeds of learning in that ground, knowing they'll have a better chance of taking root. And kids' enthusiasm won't stop at school; once they have a chance to succeed with one of their interests, that passion will spill over into other areas of their lives, forming the basis for a lifetime love of learning.

RAISE THEM UP:

Model a love of learning for young people. Let them see you taking a community education class, going to a museum, or simply reading the newspaper for pleasure.

Ask young people to use the skills they're learning in school to help you. For example, if a young person you know thinks learning math is boring or useless, ask her or him to help you create a budget for grocery shopping. Doing this not only shows young people that these skills can be useful beyond the classroom, but also gives them a sense of accomplishment.

Point out the links between education and a young person's interests whenever possible. For instance, it takes many people skilled in math, writing, drawing, electronics, and other areas to produce a video game.

horseplay

One afternoon two kids were horsing around in our building's front lobby. I had repeatedly made it clear to our program participants that horseplay—wrestling, chasing, pushing, and so on—wasn't allowed in our center's reception area.

A young girl was wrestling with a smaller boy, and during their playful tussle she accidentally pushed him against a wall. This would've been bad enough, but little did they know that the wall was made of Sheetrock. If you've ever held a piece of Sheetrock you know it's not very strong, and the scuffle left a huge hole in the wall. To make matters worse, the hole was now the very first thing visitors would see as they entered our building.

A staff member immediately phoned me and said there was an emergency in the lobby. I dropped what I was doing and rushed to the entrance. By this time a number of people had gathered. Both students and staff were hysterical over the large, jagged hole. The two guilty students were trying to compose themselves, and all eyes were on me to see how I would handle this seemingly disastrous situation.

I thought for a moment, first making a mental note to explain the difference between a "problem" and an "emergency" to my staff. Then I assessed the damage and asked the students to explain what happened. I was prepared for accusations and finger pointing, but both kids owned up to their parts in the accident. They even offered to pay to have the wall repaired.

Even though the students apologized quickly, I still wanted to use the situation to teach a lesson. At that time roughhousing in the building was a constant and troubling problem, and I was concerned about maintaining a safe environment for all of the kids. As a youth worker and parent, I'd also learned that when kids get into trouble, they'll often try to apologize just to get out of the situation as quickly as possible. I wanted these students to learn that saying you're sorry doesn't make your responsibilities go away.

I had the pair find a large piece of poster board and some markers, then asked them to make a sign that read, "This is why we do not allow horseplay in the building." When they were finished, I told them to sign their names at the bottom. After asking our maintenance person to hold off on fixing the hole, I told the students they would be responsible for standing next to the hole with the sign for the next three days after they finished their homework. This meant not only that they would be unable to participate in their usual P.A.R.K. activities, but also that every person who stepped into our building would know they were responsible for the damage.

As I watched those two young people holding the sign, it made me think about something I've heard many times from teachers, parents, and youth workers. They say, "Kids today are so immature, they play too much!" Whenever I hear statements like this I can't resist pointing out the obvious to them: kids are supposed to play! It's *how* they play that needs to be considered. I think many adults fail to make a distinction between play that is productive (games that teach kids teamwork, for example) and play that isn't, like the kind that led to the damaged wall.

If kids are primarily playing in nonproductive ways, what's the reason? One possibility is that adults aren't working to engage kids on their level. It may sound simple, but the easiest way to stop young people from doing something you don't approve of is to get them to do something else. So, if you notice kids horsing around with each other, try redirecting them by having them do something with you. If adults are more proactive about starting conversations, offering positive activity options, and praising kids when they *do* spend their time constructively, kids are likely to become more engaged and the horseplay will stop.

As for the two students who made the hole at P.A.R.K.? Well, I can't say they stopped roughhousing completely,

It may sound simple, but the easiest way to stop young people from doing something you don't approve of is to get them to do something else.

but they did go on to graduate from our program. And right up until their graduation day, they told me that they'd never forget holding the sign in front of that hole for as long as they lived.

RAISE THEM UP:

Encourage young people to participate in physical activities. Physical activity not only improves health, but also gives young people a constructive outlet for their energy. You can keep equipment (balls, jump ropes, walking shoes, music for dancing, and so on) on hand to make it even easier for kids to get moving, or if cost is a concern, explore free or low-cost opportunities in your community. Many gyms and recreation centers offer youth scholarships or sliding fee scales.

If you suspect young people are apologizing for a mistake simply to "make it go away," without understanding the consequences, have them explain to you, in their own words, why they think you're upset or concerned about the mistake. Ask them what conse- quences *they* would enact if they were adults and you were a teen.

Keep any mistakes young people make in per- spective. If necessary, take a moment to calm down before addressing the problem, then ask yourself, "Is this problem really as big as I think it is? What level of action should I/we take to solve this problem?" You'll feel less stressed and you'll be modeling effective plan- ning and decision-making skills.

kickin' it

I recently ran into three young men from the neighborhood I used to work in, and when I asked what they were up to they said, "Kickin' it." I asked the boys exactly what they were planning to do while they were "kickin' it," and they said they were going to a party. I could tell they were intoxicated, and I suspected they'd been using marijuana as well.

I asked what the term "kickin' it" meant to them, and they had trouble putting it into words—"It's just hanging out with your boys, you know, just having fun." When I pressed them further and asked what kinds of things they thought were fun, they talked about meeting girls, listening to music, and "just tripping." As they spoke the looks on their faces made it clear they didn't think an adult could possibly understand what they were talking about.

"Kickin' it" is a trend that's been going on for years. Ask many young people what they're going to do tonight, and there's a good chance they'll tell you they're "kickin' it," or "hanging out," or some variation on these. While healthy socializing is an important part of growing up, young people can easily fall into a rut of aimless (and sometimes self-destructive) hanging out and partying, and if no one intervenes they can carry the habit well into adulthood.

Most people want to have fun, and young people in particular usually have fun by spending time with their friends. Unfortunately, too often this socializing takes the form of going to parties, clubs, and bars. It's tough to expect a child who hasn't been taught to have fun in any other way to look beyond alcohol, drugs, and all the other tempting things that come with these kinds of environments. It's even harder when you think about the mixed messages the media send to kids about what it means to have fun or be "cool." Many kids I work with have the added difficulty of being left to entertain themselves. They are left alone while their parents, older siblings, and other adults go to parties and such, so they grow up waiting for the time when they can go too.

A lot of young people will tell you they feel like they *have* to be at every party, and don't want to miss a single chance to be part of "the scene." In particular, I remember talking to a 16-year-old girl who lived in a small, rural Arkansas community where there wasn't much for young people to do. The town didn't have any recreation centers or programs, and the churches were closed for most days of the week. Most kids spent their free time walking aimlessly around the town, sometimes stopping to sit and talk in the single, run-down park.

This young woman told me how eager she was to turn 18. When I asked her why, she said the security guard at the local nightclub had promised he'd let her in once she turned 18, even though the legal drinking age was 21. The sad part about this was that the thing she'd been anticipating for years, being allowed into this club, was the same thing most of the kids in that town were waiting for. Once young people turned 18, they were usually at the club whenever it was open.

"Kickin' it" in their teenage years can be a precursor to living "the fast life" or living in "the fast lane" when kids become adults. This lifestyle can sneak up on them so quickly they never see it coming. When you think about it, no young person ever starts down the road to adulthood expecting to become addicted to drugs or alcohol. But the lure of this lifestyle can be so strong that the more you try to pull them out of it, the harder it draws them back in.

Now don't get me wrong—occasional hanging out is perfectly normal. There's no need to run off and tell your kids they can never spend time with their buddies again. Just keep track of how frequently they hang out with their friends without adult supervision. Pay attention to the number of parties your child is attending, and *how* your child parties. Remember that parties these days are probably not what you remember from your own teen years. Your last memory of a party might be a bunch of kids standing around a room too scared to dance. Nowadays, if you go to a party where they're really "kickin' it," things can get pretty explicit. In my experience, alcohol abuse, violence, gambling, and sexual activity occur at these kinds of events more often than you might suspect. And don't be fooled into thinking, "My children are home almost all the time, they can't be getting into any trouble." Many young people are involved in risky activities like sex or substance abuse right under their parents' noses.

From what I've learned over the years, the most effective way to combat the lure of "kickin' it" is to show children, at as young an age as possible, other ways to enjoy themselves. As caring adults we can broaden their horizons by exposing them to positive outlets for their energy. We can help them appreciate art and expression, we can value and build on their talents, and we can let them know it's okay to be individuals and not just follow the crowd. Encourage your children to become passionate about something besides "kickin' it." If you have trouble figuring out what energizes your child, get online, look in the newspaper, or ask friends and family members for ideas. Above all, remember that just because you don't like something doesn't mean your child won't. When I was young I was fascinated with insects, which my mom couldn't stand. If they'd encouraged my interest, I might've gone into entomology or some other branch of science.

The bottom line is this: if you want to protect your children from the pitfalls of the fast life, connect with them early and often. Kids become addicted to hanging out with nothing special to do long before they become addicted to things like drugs and alcohol. And if you think it's just too hard to reach out to them, be prepared—the option of "kickin' it" will always be available to them when nothing else is.

RAISE THEM UP:

Show young people that adults can have fun without alcohol or drugs. If you're entertaining other adults in the presence of teens, have nonalcoholic options available.

If you notice young people hanging around your home or youth center with nothing special to do, engage them in a group project (like painting a room, putting on a talent show, or volunteering at a day-care center) rather than trying to interest each one in an individual activity. Young people are often influenced by their peers, and might be more inclined to participate in an activity if their friends are doing it too.

Remember, there's a difference between activities you don't find interesting or don't understand and activities you believe are actually harmful to young people. As much as possible, allow them to explore a range of safe interests, even if you don't find their choices particularly appealing.

the "unsaveable" child

There's a kid out there who scares the hell out of most youth workers. He's the kid who's been through the system. He's fearless and doesn't accept the rules. He's "unsaveable," the kid who represents the worst that can happen. Many people who work with this young person look for ways to remove him from their programs because he just doesn't seem to want the help. In fact, people get so furious when he steals or picks a fight, they could almost wring his neck.

I met a kid like this about a week into my job for Little Rock's Youth Initiative Project (YIP) as a gang intervention coordinator. Mike was about 14 years old and had already received his fair share of hard knocks from the world. His reputation preceded him—not only did my coworkers warn me about how tough he was, but some of the other young people in the program also offered words of caution.

Mike was what we in the youth-serving business call "raised by the streets," meaning he'd spent a lot of his life just hanging out with friends and older folks from his neighborhood. When I met him, he'd already been in a gang for a few years. His mouth was set in a snarl when I was introduced to him, as if to say, "Danger, beware," to anyone who dared reach out to him.

I proceeded with caution in getting to know him, and slowly but surely I began to learn some details about his background. First, he was a member of one of the most notorious gangs in the city. He was fearless, and didn't answer to anyone. Like most kids from similar backgrounds, he'd learned long before that he could make people leave him alone simply by getting angry and causing a scene.

For the first few weeks on the job I just watched him as he interacted with the center's staff. He swaggered around as if he owned the place. Most of the staff members were afraid of him, and the rest felt so sorry for him that they let him do whatever he wanted. In the end, both approaches produced the same result: a kid without any sense of boundaries or consequences.

One day a volunteer came to the center to give a presentation to some of the boys. She was a petite, well-dressed woman, and seemed like a genuinely friendly and well-intentioned person. As a professional youth worker she'd engaged with kids in a number of settings like ours, but she admitted that she'd never tried reaching out to gang-involved youth.

She tentatively began the presentation and most of the boys listened politely. After a while she grew more comfortable with the group and started to smile and relax. Then Mike eased into the room through a rear entrance, grabbing a desk right by the door. Just then, the volunteer made a comment that belittled the boys for not having any goals beyond being in a gang, adding that they had the potential to be whatever they wanted to be if they'd only set higher standards for themselves.

These boys may have made some bad choices, but they weren't fools. They each had a keen nose for disrespect and condescension. Before she could say another word, Mike lashed out at her. He loudly questioned her authority on matters of the "'hood" and her motives for being there in the first place. He demanded to know how she could begin to care about guys like them when she didn't have a clue about what their lives were like. His tirade was so merciless that the volunteer ran sobbing from the room.

In my opinion, Mike gave that volunteer a hard lesson in working with gang-involved youth. I hadn't stopped him from berating her because, unfortunately, there was truth in much of what he said. I could tell he was frustrated with people telling him what to do, just as most young people whom society labels "bad" or "worthless" feel frustrated. These kids already know right from wrong; the challenge for them is in learning how to choose between the two on their own. This was the critical point missing from the presentation.

When I asked him later why he'd challenged the speaker so vocally, he explained to me, "She ain't from around here, and she don't know $%&% about what we go through. When she first walked in the building she didn't even talk to the kids standing by the door. That's how most grown-ups are—they don't see me, they don't see any of us. It's like we're invisible."

As time went on I had more opportunities to bond with the guys in the program. Gradually they came to accept me as someone who was there to help them. They allowed me to enter their world, and as I did, I began to understand the true source of Mike's anger. By the time he was 12 he'd already been in the juvenile justice system. He wasn't very articulate and tended to need more time to process the world around him, so he ended up getting into many fights simply because he couldn't talk his way out of them. This kid lived in a world of constant violence and drama, and as a result he believed there was no place for caring or peace on the streets—only indifference, fear, brutality, and rage.

On top of all this, he was also quick-tempered. During one particular incident, I was playing football behind our building with a group of young men from the program, all members of the same gang. This was one of our regular Friday games, but on this day a group of boys from a different faction of the same gang approached us. Mike was one of them. There were about 10 boys in all, and I knew this situation could quickly get out of hand.

As they came up to us, two of the boys in that group said they needed to talk to me privately, so we walked and talked

I readily accepted the apology because I realized he hadn't been threatening me at all— he'd been lashing out at all the people who thought he was invisible, who didn't care or notice when he fell and skinned his hand.

as they led me around the side of the building. Almost immediately, out of the corner of my eye, I saw a scuffle erupt among the other boys. I ran back toward the fight and found Mike and two other boys from the rival group beating Juan, one of the boys playing football. I rushed in to pull the boys off of Juan, and as I did Mike tumbled to the sidewalk and skinned his hand. He exploded and began threatening me, spitting and cursing. He screamed to everyone listening that I was "banned from the neighborhood."

Flare-ups like this happen often in my line of work, so I wasn't surprised when he told me he was sorry the next day. I readily accepted the apology because I realized he hadn't been threatening me at all—he'd been lashing out at all the people who thought he was invisible, who didn't care or notice when he fell and skinned his hand.

These two incidents are great examples of what an important role caring adults play in the lives of young people. If that well-intentioned volunteer had spent time before her presentation getting to know the kids, asking them specific questions about their hopes and fears, she would've been in a much better position to offer them advice and encouragement. If the numerous youth workers, caseworkers, police officers, and other adults who worked with Mike had told him they believed in him, he might have been motivated to stay out of fights and work hard to live up to their high expectations. I myself wonder what might have happened to this young man if I'd had the personal and professional resources to devote more one-on-one time to him.

Instead, it took the much harsher influence of incarceration to force Mike to change his life. During a stint in prison for drug dealing, he earned his GED, studied and mastered two different trades, and learned how to control his temper—he wasn't so "unsaveable" after all. The question for parents and youth workers is this: Will you make an effort, however small, to support the young people you care about, or will you let a life sentence be the thing that rescues them?

RAISE THEM UP:

Once young people are labeled "bad" or "worthless," they often believe the reputation is permanent; this can keep them from trying to make positive life changes. Allow young people multiple chances to start fresh, even if they've made a series of bad choices or developed negative reputations over time.

Don't underestimate young people's intelligence because of their grades, appearance, or family background. Be mindful of all the ways, good and bad, that your unique stereotypes and biases affect your relationships with teens.

Showing genuine interest in young people doesn't mean you have to interrogate them or spend long hours in deep conversation. Even simple gestures like smiling and saying hello let teens know you care.

a crying place

I watched the movie *Antwone Fisher* a while back, and I felt a strong connection to it because I've seen its plot played out time and again in my work. The only difference is that I usually don't get to witness many happy endings. In my world, the boy rarely finds a home with a big, caring family and almost never gets the girl. Even less often do most of the kids I see have a caring adult in their corner like the one Denzel Washington played.

There's a scene in the movie where Antwone asks, "Who will cry for the little boy who cries inside of me?" I pondered this question for quite some time, and as a result discovered a deep well of uncried tears inside myself. They're tears I've stored up from numerous relationships with young men who've fallen victim to murder, four in the last year alone. In most cases these young men were living the life Antwone did in the movie—that of hardened gangsters.

I'll be attending a funeral later today for one of those boys, and this is what I'll see: there'll be two or three dozen young men about his age there, with cold, hard stares on their faces. Many will wear bandannas or other pieces of clothing to signify their gang allegiance. Some of them, usually the younger ones, won't be able to keep up their tough acts; they'll try and fail to hide the tears behind their hands. The boy's mother and sister will weep while his 3-year-old son looks on, completely unaware of what he's just lost. A minister will make some vague pleas about stopping the violence, but won't speak directly to anyone after the service, or even dare to step down from the pulpit until all the gang members have left. By the time we step out of the church, the boy's coffin will be covered in colorful gang artifacts. Then, a procession of cars will wind its way to the cemetery, and he'll be out of our lives forever.

The only other times we'll hear about this boy is when we run across someone from the "old neighborhood" and talk about how sad his passing was. The local news will do a quick report about a body being found, but otherwise won't acknowledge this loss of human life until the murderer is caught, or when they report on the city's crime statistics for the year. They'll say, "There were 44 homicides in Little Rock this past year," and we'll know this number includes him. After that even these small reminders will stop, replaced with new deaths and funerals.

The reason I can visualize all of this so clearly is because this is a "movie" I've seen many times over the years. But despite the store of uncried tears I carry for all these lost young men, it wasn't until a few weeks before this writing that I finally understood the question Antwone Fisher was asking. I realized it while I was attending yet another funeral for a murdered young man. The boy's best friend was there, obviously trauma-tized. His entire body was shaking with sobs, but no tears were coming out. The minister tried to console him, telling him it was okay to cry. When the boy shook his head no, the minister wrapped his arms around him and said, "Well, then I'll cry for you." And true to his word, he began to cry unashamedly. A look of stunned relief went over the boy's face, as if an enormous burden had been lifted off his young shoulders, and in a sense it had—someone else was finally taking on his pain. Other young men looked on at the weeping minister, and each one's face seemed to say, "He's crying for me too."

Right now you might be thinking, "How can I be a crying place for a young person? I'm not a minister, I'm not a professional youth worker, and I'm not a therapist. What can I do?" The main thing to remember is that while you don't always have to be a shoulder to cry on for a young person, you should try to make it safe for young people to express their feelings to you. This atmosphere of safety comes from having a good relationship, and all good relationships are built on open, positive communication. When you're talking with young people, whether it's your 5-year-old son or a 15-year-old gang member at your recreation center, remember to tell them that it's normal to make mistakes, to feel scared sometimes, and yes, to cry.

All people need a crying place, no matter how old they are, where they come from, or what decisions they've made in the past. What Antwone Fisher wanted was someone to cry for that part of him that never found a crying place. The little boy inside him desperately needed that place, but because he'd been forced to grow up so quickly he wasn't able to find it, and as a grown man he no longer knew how to cry. I think the same holds true for young people who have lived on life's hard side. They're all looking for a crying place, and for that one kind soul who is willing to feel their pain.

RAISE THEM UP:

Practice active, careful listening when you are communicating with young people. Don't interrupt or criticize a young person's ideas and opinions.

Young people need to know it's normal for people to feel afraid or confused at times, even when you're an adult. Within reasonable limits, share recollections from your own life of times when you were worried or scared. Tell young people how you handled the situation, or what you would have done differently.

The loss of a friend or relative can be very traumatic for young people. Work with them to create positive rituals that commemorate the passing of their loved ones and help provide closure. These might include writing letters to the deceased, creating a photo collage that honors them, or simply spending time talking about them with a caring adult.

the one that got away

The early nineties were a very violent time in Little Rock; there were dozens of murders every year. Many of our city's teens had chosen sides in gang turf wars. The community was in a panic, and even received national attention with the making of the HBO documentary *Gang War: Bangin' in Little Rock,* which detailed the city's gang violence through interviews, music, and video footage.

The city government hosted community forums so that concerned citizens could express their opinions and offer solutions to this epidemic. Out of those meetings came an initiative that led to the development of the Youth Initiative Project (YIP), a program designed to pull young people out of gangs, enrich their lives through positive activities, and empower them with opportunities for success. In 1995 I accepted a position with YIP as a gang intervention coordinator.

As a YIP coordinator, I was one of 12 site managers responsible for working with youth in high-risk areas throughout the city. My job was to go into gang-infested neighborhoods and recruit kids to come to my group meetings. Once everyone was there, we would talk, eat pizza, or do anything else I could come up with to engage them so they were spending less time in dangerous situations. I had to think of activities that not only appealed to younger kids but also would allow the older gang members to accept me—these older gang members had ultimate say on whether younger members were allowed to join my meetings. It was a constant negotiation process, because in this environment these kids were essentially owned by their gangs, or so it seemed. Many of these kids were so indoctrinated into this subculture that it had become a way of life, often the only one they knew.

We YIP coordinators would often organize pickup basketball and football games between our groups. One Saturday morning as I was transporting my group of guys to one of these games, I overheard a conversation between two young men, both around 13 or 14 years old.

"Are you going to the function?"

"Naw, I ain't got no money. How about you?"

"I gotta go, I missed last time. You're gonna get a V if you don't show."

"I'm gonna get one if I don't pay anyway."

"Well, what're you gonna do?"

"I don't know, man."

What these young men were talking about was whether they would attend what they called an "organizational function," or gang meeting. If you were a member of a gang you had to attend these functions whenever the gang's "council" or leaders called them. Much like in the military, higher-ranking members would pass the word down to their "lieutenants," who would in turn inform their "soldiers." The soldiers, the lowest-ranking and often youngest gang members, were then expected to attend the meeting and pay dues.

Because of their age the soldiers weren't required to contribute as much as the older members, but when you're 14 and don't have a job, any amount of money seems like a lot to pay. Even so, the threat of violence and humiliation over not paying dues was so great they would do almost anything to find the money; this usually meant selling drugs or stealing. Each lieutenant was responsible for collecting dues from his unit. He'd keep a portion for himself and pass the rest up the ladder to his superior. If any of a lieutenant's soldiers didn't pay his dues or attend a meeting, that lieutenant was responsible for assaulting the soldier on sight and covering the cost of the dues with his own money, or risk receiving similar treatment himself. This situation requires a young person to make a decision many adults will never have to make in their lifetimes.

If you've ever stopped and talked to a gang member, you'll know they're no different from any other human being; they need to belong, they want security, and so forth. But those of us who aren't in gangs tend to discount their needs because of the stigma attached to being a gang member. If they had good grades, a lot of them might find their social groups at school. If they lived in a community with a country club, they might find their niche there. But they live in areas where these groups aren't available, or they fail to meet the membership criteria. Instead, they often seek out the very obtainable entrance into "neighborhood fraternities," i.e., gangs. Then we social program workers spend countless hours and dollars trying to get them out of gangs, or, to put it another way, we try to give them different options for getting the thing they need most—a feeling of belonging.

During my time with YIP, I developed an unorthodox approach to dealing with gang members. My approach was built on the premise that a gang is any group of two or more people who gather together for a common cause. This concept forced me to look past what these young men were doing individually and to focus on the group as a whole.

I was given a chance to put this approach into action when Keith, a leading member of a local gang, was released from prison. Keith happened to be the older brother of a young man in my program. He came to me one day and asked me to help him save his little brother from the gang lifestyle, saying, "I'm a lost cause, but if you can get my brother out of this I would really appreciate it, and I'll help however I can." This concerned brother was the answer to my prayers, because he came to me at a time when I was researching this gang's founder. He'd been in a recent news article talking about a change in his personal philosophy that he wanted all the members of his gang to accept. He wanted them to make a change toward more positive activities; he said they were to stop doing drugs and terrorizing their communities and to start getting educations instead.

This was a total paradigm shift from what these young men were used to hearing, and more than a little hard for community members like me to believe. But Keith confirmed that what I'd read in the article was true. Since my program wanted the same things this founder was talking about, Keith and I worked out an agreement to try to reach those goals together. We agreed that I had the resources to spread positive information to the young gang members, and he had the influence to make them participate. We decided to hold a meeting for everyone associated with the gang. He set the meeting time and encouraged the young men to attend, while I was responsible for bringing information on positive life choices and presenting it to them. Before this partnership, attendance at my group meetings averaged about 10-20 young people per session. After Keith got involved, that number grew to about 50-60 per session.

After a few presentations from me, the boys began brainstorming community improvement projects on their own—cleaning up the neighborhood, holding a car wash to benefit a local day care, and even changing their name to promote their new positive outlook. The best part of this mass turnaround was that most of these boys were young and had a few more years of living in the neighborhood to carry out these projects, and many others.

In my youthful ignorance, I presented this new "whole-gang" approach to what was then known as Little Rock's Task Force Against Youth Violence. I proposed to the panel of community members that we institute this approach in our city-wide gang prevention efforts and direct our resources toward inclusion of the gang members by offering them a seat on the task force. Doing this would give the kids access to key decision makers while being supported by responsible adults.

My idea was greeted by smirks and stares of disbelief. One task force member sarcastically commented, "That's a great idea! And why don't we use taxpayer money to buy them bandannas and baseball caps too?" The rest of the group laughed in agreement. No one believed my proposal had merit.

In hindsight, I think the idea was so different from the tactics the task force was used to using, and the community's fear of gangs and gang members so deeply ingrained, that the idea was simply too unconventional for them to even imagine. But the worst part was still to come: telling those young people back at my program that the adults on the task force didn't want to hear about their accomplishments or champion their ideas for the future.

Without support from the wider community, my YIP sessions limped on for a couple more months until Keith was sent back to prison on a parole violation. I got another job and left YIP, and most of the boys I'd worked with quickly lost interest after that. Several years later, at 29, Keith was gunned down in a neighborhood altercation; he'd apparently gone back to the familiar life of selling drugs. The younger brother he so desperately wanted me to save was charged with capital murder in another incident.

I've realized that sometimes even though hard-to-reach kids might *want* to do something positive or proactive, adults are often guilty of holding them back, either by forbidding them outright or by not offering them support and encouragement. There are many possible reasons for this hesitation. Fear of change, whether it's a change in policies, actions, or attitudes, is often at play in these situations. In addition, the passion some adults have for helping young people can grow so strong it becomes stifling. In those instances, the adults are reluctant to allow youth to do anything on their own, for fear that they might make mistakes or come up against hard obstacles. And sometimes, the reason for not empowering youth is heartbreakingly simple—a lack of knowledge, funding, or capacity to make change happen.

I truly believe that one of the best remedies for these problems and concerns is a slow and steady approach. Maybe forming a city teen council or staging a three-day youth summit is too big for your town to contemplate right now. Instead, consider smaller events like car washes or a teen-run neighborhood block party. These events will not only give youth a chance to take the reins, but will also allow adults to see more examples of a positive teen presence in your community.

Once you have adult support, you'll have a much easier time than I did building and maintaining projects for youth. To this day, I think back on what could have been with the YIP sessions. With a little positive reinforcement from the community, that story could've had an entirely different ending.

RAISE THEM UP:

Before you get involved in a child's problems, whatever they might be, it can be helpful to do some research. For example, if the young person is in a gang, learning whatever you can about the gang's structure and rules will give you a better sense about how best to approach the situation.

Help can come from unusual places—when you're thinking about how to solve a problem in your family or community, look at *everyone* as a potential partner.

When you're working to make positive changes for young people, empower them with opportunities to contribute. Kids will be much more invested in your efforts if they feel their opinions count. In addition, young people often have creative ideas about reaching out to other young people that adults might not have.

the little boy who could've

I used to work with a kid named Devin who had a lot of influence in the streets. He was well established in the local gang and at age 14 he was giving orders to people who were much older. People respected and feared him, and he wore lots of gold jewelry and expensive clothes; in short, he was sitting firmly at the top of the neighborhood social ladder. The principal of the junior high school Devin attended once said to me, "Devin is one kid who could start a riot if he wanted," and I agreed.

I once ran into Devin and a couple of his buddies while they were skipping school. I decided to take the opportunity to explain the importance of an education, telling them that what they learned in school would stick with them long after the easy thrills of street life were gone. They in turn made a case against school, saying, "They don't want us there," and "I'm already two grades behind, so why go?" All three agreed that playing on the streets was much more fun than going to school and much more lucrative too. Devin drove the point home by pulling a wad of money from his pocket and flipping through it to show me that all the bills were hundreds. I guessed he was holding about five thousand dollars in his hand, which at the time was more than I made in two months. It left me speechless.

Despite these displays of bravado and indifference, I always believed that deep down Devin had a good heart. He loved his mother very much and had a certain magnetism that made nearly everyone gravitate toward him. When I had a chance to take a group of kids from my program to Henderson State (a nearby college) for a summer session for prospective students, I invited him to come along. The school was about an hour away from our program center in Little Rock. I would be dropping my kids off and picking them up a week later.

I stayed on for the first day to make sure the boys from my program didn't cause any trouble. The first day they played "getting acquainted" games, including a scavenger hunt and lining up by their birthdays without saying a word. It was a strange sight—the young people from other programs and schools were pretty clean-cut, while most of my boys were dressed in their traditional street gear; Devin had on his matching bandanna to boot. His pants sagged as they usually did, and he kept a menacing look fixed on his face the entire day. I could see he wasn't fitting in, and my first instinct was to take him back with me to the city. But when I told the summer session counselors about my plan, they pleaded with me to let him stay. I made it clear that I had serious doubts about leaving him there, but in the end I headed home alone. I fully expected a phone call that night because someone had made a comment that set off his temper, or because he'd snuck into a girl's room after lights out, and if neither of those things happened, I was sure they'd catch him using drugs.

To my surprise, no call came that night. I was stunned and more than a little suspicious; I drove back to the college the next day, positive I'd be taking Devin back this time. But when I got there I saw the most amazing sight—instead of fighting or sitting sullenly by himself, Devin was running up and down the halls laughing and playing with the other kids, just like a regular 15-year-old; he even had his pants pulled up! He ran up to me and started chattering about all the fun he was having. He'd gone swimming, stayed up watching movies all night with the other boys, and had already won an award for being the summer session domino champion. I was so shocked I could hardly find the words to congratulate him.

I drove home positive I'd stumbled on a way to end all gangs. Just a few days in a positive atmosphere with adults who expected him to succeed seemed to have completely changed Devin's attitude. When I came to pick the boys up a few days later, I was even more convinced—who do you think was helping the sponsors pass out the awards for the week? Yes, you guessed it. Devin was still smiling and laughing, hugging his new friends good-bye, and talking about coming back to the summer session the next year. When I saw the astonished, happy look on his face as he was handed an award for citizenship, it suddenly hit me: that tough, swaggering kid was even more surprised by the changes he'd undergone than I was.

Once the boys finished their good-byes, we piled into the van to head home. Devin sat up front with me, telling me how he was going to go to college and make something of

When I saw the astonished, happy look on his face as he was handed an award for citizenship, it suddenly hit me: that tough, swaggering kid was even more surprised by the changes he'd undergone than I was.

himself, and how amazed he'd been by how different his life was from the lives of some of the people he'd met in the past week. But as we got closer to Little Rock, he became quieter and quieter until our conversation dwindled to silence. I watched him as he stared out the window, deep in thought. He slowly reached for his bag and put his hat and gold chains back on, slouching down in the seat when he was finished. At the city limits, he pulled out his bandanna and carefully placed it around his head. When I finally reached his house, he jumped out and pulled his pants down to a comfortable sag, turned his hat to the side, and disappeared inside without saying a word to anyone.

Several years later, Devin was sentenced to an Arkansas state prison for dealing drugs. I had a chance to visit him after he was paroled, and I was surprised at both how little and how much he'd changed over the years. He was still the boy I knew back then, but there was now an air of bitterness that hung over him like a cloud. We talked briefly about the Henderson State trip. He spoke about it as though it was a pleasant but essentially unreal memory. I had the feeling he saw it as a dream or fairy tale—a detached experience that had very little to do with him.

The Henderson State experience affected me deeply because I'd caught a glimpse of what could've been. I knew that

Devin had had the potential to make a positive impact on others and himself. Unfortunately, I didn't have the resources or the forethought at the time to keep him going in a positive direction after that trip. If I had, I would have worked with him one-on-one to help him create a plan to eventually go to college, or researched other opportunities similar to the one at Henderson State that he could attend. Something to make sure the value of that week wasn't lost for him. I know now that to have lasting effects on young people, positive experiences such as that one should occur consistently over time, and not constitute just a few days out of a teen's entire life.

I also took another valuable lesson away from that summer—learning to see these Henderson State experiences in all kids. To this day, when I meet young people who seem lost or headed down the wrong path in life, I immediately try to imagine how they might be affected if they were at Henderson State, or in some other environment that allowed them to just be kids and play while empowering them to take control of their lives.

The thing I hope you take away from this story is that most of the kids you're dealing with, however hardened they seem, need a Henderson State experience at some point in their lives, and they need consistent, supportive follow-up afterward to maintain its benefits. They need a chance to be exposed to young people who are doing different things, or at the very least to know that there's a world beyond their block or neighborhood.

RAISE THEM UP:

Don't underestimate the power of examples when talking with kids. It's often easier for young people to dream about the future when they have concrete examples to base their goals on. Expose young people to as many positive adult role models as possible, whether it's one of your coworkers, a member of your congregation, or another staff member at your youth center.

 A change of scenery can have a profound effect on a teen, and it doesn't have to come from an expensive trip. Even a bus ride to a part of town they don't normally visit can give young people a fresh perspective on life.

Keep your expectations of kids high and watch them respond to prove you right.

when grown-ups can't reach me

Many young people have told me over the years that they don't think adults really understand them. You might have experienced a similar feeling when you were younger. It can seem like kids and adults speak totally different languages! Examples of the communication gaps are everywhere: kids have their interests, adults have theirs, and the two rarely seem to intersect. Adults get flustered when kids don't see things the way they'd like them to, or act in ways they think are strange or downright offensive.

Kids become angry because they want more independence and think adults are withholding it unfairly.

Despite the hurdles, caring adults have to find ways to say the things we want kids to hear in a language they can understand. This means we have to learn which ideas, words, and images will have the most impact on them; encourage them at an early age to speak their minds openly and honestly; and make concrete plans for how to talk to kids before we find ourselves in a crisis situation. Following these three steps isn't always easy and won't make your relationships with kids perfect overnight, but it will help you lay a solid foundation for respectful communication with the young people you care about.

The first step, learning about what makes young people tick, can be uncomfortable because it may involve some compromise on your part. I once witnessed a situation where a little effort to learn about kids and a little compromise would've gone a long way. I was a member of the planning committee for a teen conference. The goal of the conference was to present several workshops to hard-to-reach teens on various issues affecting them. One of the workshops in particular focused on teaching young men the value of respecting women. We were hoping to have two or three boys act as panel members.

During one planning session, a colleague and I argued about how best to deliver this workshop's message. She believed we should choose young men who were relatively "clean-cut"—youth ministers, student government leaders, Boy Scouts, and so on. Her point was that we needed to choose young people who would act as role models to the teens attending the workshop. I agreed with her in principle, but thought we should first look at the message we wanted to deliver (the importance of respect for women) and then look at who would be receiving that message (a group of teenage boys— a pretty tough audience under the best circumstances). I proposed that we choose kids who looked like the kids we were presenting the information to, which in this instance meant wearing baggy pants, earrings, and all the trappings of that particular youth population. I explained that in my experience, kids in general tended to pay attention to people they could relate to.

The committee ultimately decided to go with my colleague's choice. At the last minute, however, the young man she'd chosen wasn't able to make it to the workshop. One of the boys attending from my program volunteered to go up on stage to be part of the panel of speakers. He was so articulate and passionate about the topic that he quickly became the dominant speaker on the panel. As I looked around the audience of engaged, excited teens, all I could think about was how much better the workshop might have been if the young man I'd brought had known he was going to speak beforehand.

Think about this story when you're trying to connect with kids. If it's important that a young person gets the information you're presenting then use the best means available to deliver that message, even if it's dressed in a way you don't necessarily approve of. Connecting with kids may mean having to go to a ball game or pizza place with kids and their buddies. It may mean listening to a little of their music or watching their favorite television shows to find some conversation starters. Worst of all, it may even mean telling kids a few embarrassing stories about your own youth to try to find common ground. Don't get discouraged or self-conscious. Keep in mind that having these kinds of casual interactions doesn't just teach you how to talk to young people; it also helps create an environment that's beneficial for talking in general. Think about it: if you find yourself only communicating with kids to punish or criticize them, or when you're discussing a "big" issue like sex or grades, they'll get used to talking to you in that way and be less likely to see you as a confidant and ally. On the other hand, when young people are used to talking to you about all sorts of issues—big and little, good and bad— they'll find it easier to open up to you in general, and you'll be more comfortable communicating with them as well.

One thing adults should keep in mind when learning about young people is that no matter how cool you once were as a teen or how "with it" you think you are now, you're still an adult and come from an entirely different era of youth culture than the one kids live in today. Things like acceptable behavior, slang, attitudes, and so on are evolving all the time. Adults must understand this and adjust their communication strategies accordingly. Remember, getting through to them isn't about trying to fit into their world as much as it is about understanding and respecting their world. It's also important to realize that kids have to process a lot of conflicting information from countless sources. They are trying to navigate the formal and informal rules of schools and communities. They are listening to peers, teachers, coaches, celebrities, and everyone else who has a position of influence in their lives. This means your voice can sometimes get lost in the noise of their day-to-day lives.

The second key step in getting through to kids is establishing a pattern early on of allowing young people to speak their minds. Some things, whether it's how chores are divided between family members or when and where homework gets done, should be up for discussion, giving young people a voice in the

The last thing any caring adult wants is to be caught off-guard when a young person needs help the most.

things that affect them. Even everyday conversations can be opportunities to empower kids. When you're talking, remember that adults don't always have to lead the conversation, and by no means should they have all the answers. For example, the workshop I mentioned before had an adult facilitator to make sure the panel didn't get off-track. But since the young man I brought was such a charismatic speaker, the adult didn't need to do much facilitating. In my opinion, this made for a much more lively discussion among the teens and made each participant feel more engaged in the workshop in general.

Finally, getting through to young people is much easier when you've established a concrete goal for what it is you are trying to accomplish. Setting a goal includes planning what you want to say in advance and figuring out the best possible time to say it. When you have a clear idea of what it is you want a young person to understand, you'll have a better idea of the number of different roads that will get you there and you'll have an easier time getting the words out. For instance, if my 6-year-old son decides someday to engage in underage drinking in his teens, I'm already planning to tell him about the times during my own teen years when I came home drunk from parties and spent the whole night throwing up into the toilet. I know that to keep him from running into the same mistakes I did, I have to give him useful information in a way he'll understand. I also know that thinking about this potential problem now will make me much more comfortable dealing with it if it comes up later. The last thing any caring adult wants is to be caught off-guard when a young person needs help the most.

A father I knew told me about a time when advance planning would've helped him talk to his teenage son. The son had been caught smoking marijuana a number of times, which came as a shock to the father. Without any plan in place, he fell back on arguing with his son and lecturing him on the dangers of drugs. Whenever they talked, the son would listen and seem to understand what his dad was saying—only to get in trouble again for using drugs soon after. Then the father had an idea. First, he had his son spend time talking with an old friend of his who'd lived a rough life because of drug abuse. Then he took the boy to some of the down-and-out places he himself had frequented as a teen. While visiting these old haunts they had a chance to talk to a number of people whose lives had been ruined because of drug abuse, forcing the boy to face the concrete evidence of drugs' destructive powers head-on. The boy was very affected by the experience because there was no denying the similarities between his life and the stories he heard. He immediately made the decision to stop using drugs because of what he'd witnessed. The point here is that the father stepped out of his comfort zone and made an intentional effort to speak in a language his son could understand, even though it meant admitting to some less-than-perfect decisions he'd made in the past. If he'd taken the time to devise this plan earlier, before the problem ever came up, he might have saved himself and his son a great deal of conflict and heartache.

Working through these steps of learning, empowering, and planning may seem hard now, but the relatively short-term work you do today will give you the benefits of enhanced communication with the kids you care about for years to come.

One of the easiest ways to empower kids is by giving them meaningful responsibilities. Ask teens to tutor young children in reading, take charge of organizing an event, or be responsible for planning and preparing one family dinner each week.

Learning about a young person's interests can be more fun for both of you if you share recollections about your own teen years. Compare favorite songs, popular dances, hairstyles, and other things that have changed since you were a teenager.

When you're having a conversation with a teen, try asking questions that require more than a yes or no answer. For instance, you might ask, "If you could live anywhere in the world, where would it be?" or "What would you change about our community (neighborhood, school, etc.) if you could?"

bust a flow

I was mowing my lawn late one summer evening
when I saw two young men walking up the street
toward me. They looked about 13 or 14 years old.
One was rapping while the other was grooving
to the beat, bobbing his head in time.

As the two boys got closer I could make out the words
of the rap—it was riddled with some pretty vulgar profanity.
Watching them walk past my yard I wondered if the young
rapper would stop swearing once he noticed an adult watching
him. In fact, he did just the opposite—the second he saw me,
he starting shouting the lyrics even louder, looking me right in
the eye as if to say, "What are you going to do about it?"

Feeling totally disrespected, I decided to make the boys stop using profanity around me. I called to them to come over for a minute. They stopped and stood there hesitantly, so I added, "You want to make a couple of dollars?" Now I had their attention. They started walking slowly toward me, looking as if they were ready to turn around and run the second I asked them to mow my lawn or do some other chore.

"You think you can flow, don't you?" I asked the rapper. He straightened up with pride. "For sure."

"Well, I didn't like the song you were singing, so I'd like to challenge you to a rap battle. We'll each rap for 30 seconds without using any profanity, and your friend here can be the judge. If you win, I'll give you five dollars and do 50 push-ups right here. If I win, you have to finish mowing my lawn and promise not to use any profanity for the rest of the day. We have a deal?"

He looked me up and down carefully, as if he was taking my measure. "You got a bet, old man. You first."

I launched straight into a favorite rap that I use for just such occasions. The song had been popular when I was in my 20s so the boys were too young to remember it. They nodded along in approval, and when I was finished they politely gave me my props. Then it was his turn.

This young boy proceeded to unleash a barrage of lyrical bullets so strong my jaw nearly dropped to the ground. I was floored, not only by his ability to rap but by the way he improvised a storyline for his song that didn't use one word of profanity. He even went past the required 30 seconds and kept going for more than a minute with ease. When he finished, I didn't wait for his friend to declare a winner. I graciously handed over the five dollars, dropped to the ground, and did 50 push-ups in the street. Both boys laughed while I did the push-ups, and when I stood up the rapper smiled and said, "Any time you have some money you want to get rid of just let me know, Old School."

To my surprise he stayed and talked with me. I gave him some advice about honing his musical ability and told him to work on producing songs that didn't need cursing to sound good. We ended up chatting for nearly 20 minutes before they headed off down the sidewalk.

About a month or so later I was out in my yard and the rapper happened to pass by again, this time with a different friend. He remembered me from that day and he stopped to talk with me for a few minutes. He performed several of his newer songs, some of which had positive themes and didn't contain a single swear word.

I believe the thing that helps me bridge the gap between adults and young people is that I try not to be judgmental, I have a genuine interest in what teenagers are doing, and I don't mind putting aside my pride and being silly once in a while if I think it's going to engage them. Those boys in particular were impressed by the fact that I accepted their music and was willing to take the time to offer them advice. I also have high expectations for how young people should act. I've found that when I let teens know that I expect them to be respectful of adults, their peers, and their community in general, most times they'll respond by doing just that. In return, I give them the same respect of their abilities, opinions, and basic humanity that I would want.

To this day I consider those five dollars among the best I've ever spent. I may have lost a little money out of my wallet, but I hope that I made an investment in my community that will be much more valuable than money in the long run.

As an adult, you have much more to offer young people than you might think. When you're trying to make connections with teens, don't think any hobby, skill, or experience you have is too silly or boring to interest them. You might be pleasantly surprised to discover common interests.

Remember the Golden Rule by treating young people the same way you would like to be treated. Just because they're younger than you doesn't mean teens don't deserve the same respect and civility you would give to an adult.

Everyone who lives in a community plays a part in affecting its *climate*—another word for the general "feel" of a place. You can affect the climate in a positive way (bringing dinner to a sick neighbor), in a negative way (spraying graffiti on a storefront), or in a neutral way (by keeping to yourself and not speaking to anyone on your block). How do you want to affect *your* community's climate?

snotty-nosed kids

I am the proud father of two beautiful boys who, as I am writing, are 3 and 6. When my sons were babies, strangers would come up to me on the street and comment on how cute they were. Whether we were at the mall, in a grocery store, or at the park, grandmothers and teenagers alike would ask to hold them or play with them. I even joked with friends that people were usually nicer to me just because I was with the boys!

One of the greatest joys in the world for me is to hug and get hugged by my kids. It just melts me. I feel so wonderful when they run to greet me and give me that unconditional hug that just says, "I love you, Dad." Those hugs are especially good after a long day, when it feels as if the world has just finished chewing me up and spitting me out. I've often thought about how beneficial it must be for adults to receive those kinds of hugs from kids. I think it makes each one of us better and, in some way, makes the whole world a kinder, more positive place.

I had an interesting experience with hugs while taking my younger son to day care. One morning we arrived at the day-care center at our usual time. I unbuckled him from his car seat and grabbed him up with a tight daddy-loves-you hug. I carried him into the building and as I put him down and turned to leave, I noticed another child standing nearby. She looked to be about 1 year old and was covered in what smelled like chocolate or some other sticky stuff. She also had a very runny nose. She looked up from the toy she was playing with and caught my eye, and wouldn't you know it, she made a beeline toward me as if she was going to try to stop me from leaving. At that point in my parenting career, I knew enough about groups of toddlers to know there could be a bad scene if one of them got upset. I hurriedly said my good-byes and made a move toward the door. But just then, she looked up at me with her beautiful brown eyes and stretched out her arms in that nonverbal way that says, "Pick me up!"

This wasn't a distraction I had time for; I was on my way to work. Besides that, I was wearing a starched white shirt, my favorite tie, and pressed slacks. Needless to say, I was a little cleaner than the sticky, wiggly bundle of arms and legs standing in front of me.

Just then, I had a realization that forever changed the way I see kids, and people in general for that matter. In that moment of wondering how to get out of that situation,

I thought about how many other parents had dropped their kids off that day and made it out the door before she was able to catch them. Had she been successful in getting even one hug? Even worse, had anyone noticed before I did that she was there and wanted to be picked up?

Then I thought about how many other kids have grown up in exactly the same circumstances. The snotty-nosed kids everyone ignores today tend to grow up into the "problem children" of tomorrow. These kids may not have dirty noses and chocolate all over them anymore, but they might have intimidating tattoos or saggy pants, drink and do drugs, or just have a bad attitude and filthy mouth. They've been used to being outcasts for so long, to having people cross the street when they see them coming, that many of them figure they might as well live up to the reputation they've been saddled with. Their pleas for hugs and attention and respect have been passed up so many times before that putting up a tough exterior has become an automatic defense against feeling rejected.

When this little girl reached for me, I saw all of those rejected kids in her face. I picked her up, kissed her on the cheek, and said, "You're okay." She gave me a wide grin that made me forget all about my clean clothes. Then, just as quickly as she'd run into my arms, she motioned for the floor and ran away to play. When I inspected myself to assess the damage, guess what I found? Not a single speck of dirt anywhere. As I was going out the door, I looked back to see her waving at me alongside my son, as if they were both saying, "We love you, Daddy."

Even though the moment was short-lived, it left me feeling as if my heart had grown 10 times bigger. The experience gave me a new perspective on reaching out to kids, and made me realize that a single hug goes a long way and that it's important for adults to care for all kids, not just our own. I know my sons have a great support system in place—they have two loving parents, a large extended family, and all sorts of family friends and well-wishers. But I can't just think about them. I learned that I also have to think about the kids next door, the ones who need someone looking out for them too. I have to think about these kids if for no other reason than that they might one day be the ones influencing my sons. If I've neglected them all along, when they're older they might become the kids I don't want hanging around with my boys. As far as I can tell, the best thing I can do to prevent that is to start including them in the love now.

I can start extending care and concern to these kids by not getting upset when they're always at my house wanting something to eat, or won't go home because there's no one there to look after them. I can give them the same rewards I give my sons for hard work and integrity, and help them learn the things I want my own children to learn. I can then stretch a little further and try to be supportive to all the kids in my neighborhood. I can put up a basketball hoop in front of my house, I can help organize a kid-friendly event, or I can just make my house a place that's welcoming to young people. What if I was the dad the other kids came to for advice, or the one who always dropped them off at practice or the movies? Then I could teach other adults how to be caring role models for the neighborhood as well, and, if we're lucky, all of those snotty-nosed kids will grow up knowing they are loved.

RAISE THEM UP:

Play favorites—with *all* the young people you know. Extend respect, concern, and attention to each one.

Take (reasonable) risks when you're interacting with young people. For example, try introducing yourself to a neighborhood child you don't know, or writing a thank-you note to the teenager who bags your groceries at the supermarket. Taking steps out of your comfort zone will help you learn more about yourself and show the young person how rewarding it can be to try new things.

Don't be afraid to get a little sticky—model respect and fairness by refraining from judging young people by their outward appearances.

validation

Think back to a time when you were recognized. Maybe it was for a special achievement at work, or because you gave a family member a thoughtful birthday present, or maybe it was just for being a good friend. Were you excited to get that positive appreciation, or did you not really notice the praise at all?

For many of us validation comes in so many different forms and from so many people that we tend to take it for granted. For example, when I scored points on my high school basketball team I took the cheering crowds for granted. I didn't realize it at the time, but it was those cheers that boosted my confidence and self-esteem, not the points I made.

Validation is so powerful that it makes a positive impact even when it comes from a less-than-ideal source. When I was a child in Houston, Texas, one of the more notorious characters on my block (a known drug dealer and car thief) would always go out of his way to praise me. Whenever I passed by the corner he frequented, he would say to everyone in earshot, "Hey look everybody, here comes my main man Moody!" My chest would puff up with pride as all the guys on the corner laughed and teased me.

The need for recognition comes in a variety of forms. In my 1st-grade class there was a boy who was given the "title" of being able to beat up everybody else, and outrun all of us too. This was a badge of honor of sorts for this boy, because he was good at something and other kids looked up to him for it. I also remember the girl we all thought was the prettiest in the class. The boys validated her by fighting for the honor of her affection. Even the kid who was the slowest runner and never had new clothes or toys could still feel proud because he was the best at drawing. Somehow, without knowing what we were doing or why, our class managed to find ways for each person to shine.

We all want a place in the world where we can make a significant contribution and be applauded by our peers. This is very evident in most inner-city communities, where youth often choose the lure of gangs or other risky activities in hopes of getting the positive attention they don't receive in other parts of their lives. In particular, I remember the case of a young man named Troy at my center. Troy was going through a rough patch—getting into a lot of trouble in school, in the neighborhood, and at home. When I spoke with his mother, she said he'd been acting strangely. His teachers noticed how aggressive he'd become in class, as if he was angry at the whole world. One day he was ushered into my office by a staff member, who said, "Troy's just not into today" (meaning he was refusing to do any work). I could tell right away how frustrated he was—he barely said hello and couldn't bring himself to look me in the eye.

We all want a place in the world where we can make a significant contribution and be applauded by our peers.

This was familiar territory for me, so I used one of my favorite approaches for talking with unhappy kids. I began casually chatting about anything but the topic we were there to deal with. I asked which team his school's basketball team was playing this week, how his girlfriend was doing—any little thing to make him comfortable and get him talking. Slowly but surely he started to look at me, answer questions, and even offer additional comments. I knew then that he was open and ready to discuss the matter at hand.

He first explained that he was just having a tough time that day, and didn't think it was such a big deal if he didn't feel like working. I told him I felt the same way too sometimes; we all have days when we feel a little down. I suggested we go outside and take a short walk to clear our heads. As we walked, an idea suddenly occurred that I hadn't considered before: asking him what it was like being a middle child. I knew Troy had an older sister and a younger brother. I grew up as the middle child too, so I knew exactly how hard it can be to feel special in that situation.

To Troy, that doorknob represented a chance to gain the confidence and praise he'd been yearning for his entire life, for him to feel he'd made a contribution to the world, or at least to the mother he adored.

His eyes widened in amazement and I could almost hear the floodgates opening inside of him. His words tripped over each other as he explained how good his older sister was at everything, while he could barely cross the street on his own. With tears in his eyes he said, "It just seems like I can never do anything right. She's got all types of awards on her wall and I don't even have one." He started crying. "Last week I fixed the handle on my mom's bedroom door. She acted like it was no big deal, even though it took me forever!" To Troy, that doorknob represented a chance to gain the confidence and praise he'd been yearning for his entire life, for him to feel he'd made a contribution to the world, or at least to the mother he adored.

I comforted Troy as best I could, telling him how impressed I was with his ability to fix things. I also gently explained that sometimes people, even deserving ones, didn't always get validation for their good works. In these cases people had to be their own cheerleaders. Troy came away from the conversation feeling better, knowing that at least one person valued the unique contributions he gave to the world.

Even now, as a fairly confident adult, I'm still surprised by just how strong the human need for approval can be. I received firsthand evidence of this when I was asked to deliver a motivational speech on finding your passion to a group of teenagers at a local youth center. I'd given talks on this topic before, so I felt comfortable on the stage. During the speech I could tell the kids were listening and interested, and in general I thought I was doing a good job. But when I finished and stepped down from the stage, only a few of the young people in the audience stopped and thanked me for coming. I was confused and more than a little concerned. I usually had to excuse myself as audience members tried to tell me long stories about their personal lives or stopped me to exchange phone numbers. I left the center somewhat discouraged because this group hadn't validated my effort.

Later that week, I was lying on my sofa watching the Olympics on television. It was a medal ceremony for one of the events. I studied the athletes' faces as they accepted their hard-earned awards. They shouted and cried tears of joy, hugging their teammates when they stepped down from the podiums. It seemed as if they were speaking a universal language, one that was built on the happiness that comes from being acknowledged as the best in the world. I imagined that Pulitzer Prize winners, Oscar-winning actors, and Super Bowl champions probably felt exactly the same way, even if they didn't shout or cry. Badges, certificates, trophies, and so on are important to us because they say to the world, "For that moment, I was appreciated and I mattered."

When I thought about that speech I'd given, I realized I still felt confident I'd done a good job. The only reason I felt disappointed was because no one had taken time to tell me so. I quickly got over my bruised ego because I'd been in that situation before. I knew my speechwriting skills, while func-tional, always had room for improvement, and that I would have other chances to practice them in the future. But the fact remains—everyone, including me, wants validation.

When you're dealing with troubled youth, even the ones who act as if they couldn't care less what you think of them, remember the story of Troy and the doorknob. The key to getting through to them might be as simple as saying, "Good job," or "I appreciate you."

RAISE THEM UP:

Be creative in rewarding young people for positive actions—recognition doesn't have to take the form of tangible prizes or treats. For example, you might create a bulletin board at your youth center to visually showcase young people's achievements, or make up a special cheer to say whenever someone in your family has a success.

Sometimes adults don't realize how many negative things they say to young people. Try this easy test: for one day keep a mental or written tally of the number of negative and positive comments you make to the young people around you. If at the end of the day you find you're making many more negative comments than positive ones, make a conscious effort to use more positive words in the future.

Look for positive actions in unusual places and recognize them enthusiastically. A young person might get average grades in school but volunteer at a homeless shelter every weekend. Congratulate their humanitarian efforts while coaching them to greater academic success.

balloons over chicago

As the son of divorced parents, I made many
trips back and forth between my mother in Texas
and my father in Illinois. When I was about 12
years old, visiting my father on the north side of
Chicago, he decided it was time for me to have
a summer job. For the next three months I would
go out with him on Saturday mornings to sell
balloons on the street. Unlike some kids, I was
thrilled by the prospect of working alongside my
father. I figured that not only could I make a
decent amount of money to put toward school

clothes for me and my little sister, but I'd also get to meet a lot of interesting people with the comfort of knowing my dad was right there beside me. As far as I was concerned, it was a win-win proposition for both of us.

I didn't know it at the time, but I would get much more out of the job than money and new friends. My father was teaching me something that would go on to benefit me for the rest of my life: the art of survival, of using the abilities and resources I had to create something out of nothing.

I followed along that summer as he mentored me. First he showed me how to get to the warehouse where I'd rent my helium tanks. Then he bought me a push dolly for carting the tank around. He took me to a store that gave the best deals on balloons and taught me how to price them so I'd make a profit. He also gave me advice on handling people. I learned at an early age that the most important thing in business was to keep the customers happy.

Watching my father work with people fascinated me. He would never hesitate to give customers another balloon if they said the one they'd bought had blown away or popped. He didn't even bother to question them, even when it seemed obvious to me they were lying. Some of his best customers would occasionally get two or three balloons for the price of one, just for being regulars. But more than friendly service and free balloons, I noticed how he would always take time to listen to the people who came by. He would go out of his way to engage people in conversation to keep our balloon stand looking busy and inviting. At 12 years old, I was getting an education in hard work, respect, and teamwork that I have just now begun to fully appreciate.

The next summer, when I returned to take my post alongside Dad at his balloon stand, he told me things were going to be a little different that summer: I was being promoted. Instead of helping out at his stand I would now be managing a nearby corner of my own. On the first day he drove me to my new post, stayed for a couple of hours to make sure I had a handle on things, then left. He came by a few times throughout the day to check on me and let me take breaks, but I was otherwise working alone.

At 12 years old, I was getting an education in hard work, respect, and teamwork that I have just now begun to fully appreciate.

At first I was terrified at being left out on the streets of Chicago by myself, but after a while I got used to it. After all, I knew Dad would be coming back to see how I was doing. I even caught him watching me from across the street a couple of times. While I was out there on my own, I learned to solve problems because I had no other choice. I learned to negotiate and deal with people. When my father returned at the end of each day, we'd discuss the situations that had come up during the day and he'd give me advice on how to handle them next time.

This went on for a couple of weeks until I was promoted again. Now my father was just going to drop me off in the mornings and not come back until pick-up time. Again, this was tough at first, because now I had to figure out how to take breaks by myself. I could no longer rely on my father being there to take over for me when I got tired. But like before, I eventually figured out how to manage my time and make sure the balloon stand was secure when I needed to step away for a minute. This was a major growing point for me because this new responsibility forced me to work through some major fears and helped me experience personal success. I went home for the summer with an immense feeling of pride and a good-sized wad of money in my wallet.

When I turned 14 the next summer, I was ready to pick up where I'd left off. Dad informed me that things had, naturally, changed again. He was working at a different job now, and his employers didn't offer a lot of flexibility when it came to hours. This meant he wouldn't be able to drop me off or pick me up at my stand. I felt this would be another opportunity for me to grow and I accepted the challenge. Instead of getting a ride from my dad I now had to catch two trains and a bus, and then walk a good distance to a storage facility near the Lincoln Park Zoo. After picking up my supplies, I would open shop every morning. I worked until about six o'clock in the evening and then packed up and followed the same route home.

I sold balloons (and eventually T-shirts, umbrellas, and other items) in Chicago well into college. I eventually quit when various obligations, like schoolwork and marriage, began to take up more of my time. To this day, I can't pass by a balloon stand without feeling a sense of both nostalgia and accomplishment.

When I tell people about my summers selling balloons, some react by saying, "What was your father thinking, putting you in charge of all that money by yourself?" Others assume I must've been a model child for Dad to entrust me with so much responsibility. Well, I can tell you I was by no means a perfect kid. As for what my father was thinking, I couldn't say. But whatever his intentions, I believe that he gave me an opportunity to rise to a challenge and overcome my fears about talking to strangers and resolving problems on my own. Rather than assume I couldn't be left alone or figure out how to solve problems without his help, he gave me the chance to struggle and succeed.

Today, I use the skills I learned at that balloon stand (salesmanship, diplomacy, organization, public speaking, and so on) in nearly every aspect of my professional and personal life. Learning how to receive rejection from people who didn't buy balloons without taking it personally helped me develop the self-confidence I need as a youth worker and parent. But most importantly, the chance my father gave me then bolstered not only the trust I have in myself, but also my ability to trust the young people I work with every day.

RAISE THEM UP:

♥ The same young person who rebels against you might eagerly work to impress another adult. So even if you believe a teen wouldn't do well in an after-school job, give it a try. Talk with other adults you know and ask if they could use any extra help in their homes or workplaces.

☺ As a caring adult, your first instinct when giving young people new responsibilities might be to hover nervously around them. Whenever possible, give them room to solve problems and, yes, make a few mistakes. You'll be expressing your trust in them and they'll get valuable practice in independent decision making.

☺ Some young people thrive when they are thrown into new situations, while others require more time to get used to change. Always take your cues from young people when gauging their comfort level with new things, whether it's new jobs, friends, or places.

never give up

If you're raising a teenager or working with teens
on a regular basis, you've probably at one time
or another reached the point where you just want
to throw in the towel. It might've come the time
they broke a neighbor's window, went to jail, got
caught having sex, stole money, or snuck out—
whatever it was, it probably made you want to just
send them away to let someone else try to handle
them. You probably felt angry, embarrassed,
hurt, and maybe ashamed. You thought you'd
taught them better, that your positive influence

was having some effect, and you couldn't figure out why they were acting like this.

I think there's a time and place when adults can give up. If you are playing dominoes, charades, or video games, then by all means feel free to call it a day whenever you feel like it! But giving up on a child is not an option. Look at it this way: if you decide to give up on teens, what will happen when they have no one to answer to? How will your reactions during a moment of anger and stress resonate throughout their lives?

⁜

I once worked with a 13-year-old boy who, in my opinion, was a good kid. He didn't get into any major trouble in school or at home and had a very involved mother in his life. But he started hanging out with some of the neighborhood thugs. These guys accepted him with open arms, no prerequisite. All he had to do was show up. As time went on, the kinds of activities they were involved in started to change from simple youthful mischief to actual crimes.

By the time he was 15, this boy was a full-fledged member of his neighborhood gang. He accepted his newfound status as a badge of honor and quickly began climbing the ranks by doing things that would help him earn a reputation as a hardened criminal. His mother didn't understand the world her son had entered and couldn't figure out how to get him back. In her frustration and fear she began to fight constantly with her son, and the more she fought, the deeper he sank into this world. Then one day I got a call at around 2:00 A.M. She'd decided she had no other choice but to put her 15-year-old son out of the house and into the streets of southwest Little Rock, Arkansas.

I allowed the boy to stay with me that night, but the next day he had to go home. He wasn't old enough for his mother to put him out, and he hadn't broken any laws. When he turned 16 the following year she booted him out again, saying she simply didn't have the energy or resources to deal with him anymore. Well of course he went right to the streets that loved him and started making money to support himself. He sold drugs like most of his peers, primarily marijuana and crack cocaine, and ended up with a few minor criminal charges.

Unfortunately the threat of a prison sentence wasn't enough to stop him and he continued dealing drugs. By this time he was also smoking marijuana and drinking heavily on a regular basis. The more drugs he sold and used the more he was accepted into the ranks of the gang, which meant he now had a status as a hard-core gang banger that required constant maintenance.

I found out eventually that this young man was sentenced to 10 years in the Arkansas Department of Corrections. I remember thinking when I learned of his fate that prison, sadly, was probably a good thing for this kid; at least it meant he wouldn't be gunned down in the streets. Soon afterward I ran into his mother in a local grocery store. I could tell she'd been crying, and she looked completely exhausted. I asked how her son was doing, and with tears in her eyes she said, "Okay, considering." I told her I'd heard about his 10-year prison sentence and figured he'd probably only end up serving 3 or 4 years with good behavior. A pained look crossed her face. "No, my baby got 60 years." Apparently he'd been back to court on more serious charges since I'd last heard about him. This mother now had to live with the daily anguish of knowing her

I think there's a time and place when adults can give up. If you are playing dominoes, charades, or video games, then by all means feel free to call it a day whenever you feel like it! But giving up on a child is not an option.

son was being raised by convicts, which was horrible enough to imagine. But the thing that struck me the most from the conversation was when she said, "The pain I went through when he was 15 years old and rebelling against my authority was nothing compared to the pain I'm dealing with now."

This story may seem like an extreme example to use, but I believe the lesson it offers applies to everyone who's ever thought about giving up on a child: young people need consistent and positive support from adults to help them thrive. This is equally true in good times and bad times, and it's true even when it seems as if the last thing a teen needs or wants is your help. So when caring for a young person feels like an uphill struggle, remember how important the support you're giving now will be in the future, and keep your eye on the prize.

RAISE THEM UP:

Whenever you feel discouraged about the young people you care about, remind yourself of their positive skills and actions. Perhaps an aggressive teen is also very loving and protective of a younger sibling, or a young person who frequently skips school happens to be a talented writer. Keeping these positive qualities in mind can help you remember why it's important to support young people even when they seem irredeemable.

Focus your energies on what really matters. For example, teens' clothing choices, while mystifying to you, aren't likely to stay the same forever and probably don't warrant a daily battle. But drug abuse can have negative consequences for the rest of their lives and requires your immediate attention.

♥ Recognize that you can't and shouldn't be everything to a young person. Knowing when you need help dealing with a hard-to-reach teenager, whether it's from a counselor, social worker, religious figure, or someone else, is a sign not of weakness but of maturity and strength.

raise them up:

6 Bonus Tips for Connecting with Hard-to-Reach Youth

1 **Practice makes perfect.** When you care about a hard-to-reach young person, often the only thing that's certain is uncertainty. You might find yourself having to do a lot of thinking on your feet, which is a challenge to many people. To get more comfortable with quick thinking, practice working through possible situations before they arise by asking "What if?" questions. For example, "What if I suspected my daughter was using drugs? How would I respond?" Come up with a variety of ideas to keep handy, just in case.

2 **Don't forget that every young person has value.** Young people are like $100 bills: whether a bill is crumpled, dirty, or slightly torn, it still has worth. Keep reminding yourself to look beyond a teen's outward appearances for the unique and valuable person within.

3 **Talk to them early and often.** Start asking questions before any signs of trouble, not when a problem is already far advanced. Keep talking to teens—don't expect their problems to "just go away" or "clear up on their own."

4 **Don't expect young people to reach out to you.** Take the initiative as an adult to reach out to them, and don't take it personally if your attempts aren't immediately reciprocated. Young people, especially those who have been rejected or ignored before, can find it hard to open up to adults.

5 **Take care of yourself.** Taking care of your own health (physical and mental) will not only give you the energy and determination to get through the tough times you experience with young people, but will also give them a role model of the healthy, responsible adult you want them to be. One way you can help yourself is by asking for help from other adults when you need it. Remember, you don't have to do all the work of building relationships with kids on your own.

6 **Be clear and consistent.** When you have boundaries and rules for young people, whether they apply to your home, recreation center, or congregation, make sure to create clear consequences for breaking those rules as well. Explain these rules and consequences early on in your relationship and stick to them.

150 Ways to Show Kids You Care (Los Niños Importan: 50 Maneras de Demostrár selo). Even the simplest acts of kindness can build assets in the lives of children. This warm, inviting bilingual book provides 150 easy ideas and meaningful reminders about how adults can show kids they really care.

"Ask Me Where I'm Going" & Other Revealing Messages from Today's Teens. This intimate little book will touch your heart as you read poignant and practical "real words" from teens describing what they want from the caring adults in their lives.

Conversations on the Go: Clever Questions to Keep Teens and Grown-Ups Talking by Mary Ackerman. This stimulating, go-anywhere book gives teens and adults a chance to find out what the other one thinks. Filled with intriguing questions, some deep and some just fun, it's guaranteed to stretch the imagination and bring out each other's personality and true self.

Just When I Needed You: True Stories of Adults Who Made a Difference in the Lives of Young People written and edited by Deborah Fisher. *Just When I Needed You* is a hope-filled collection of stories from adults who remember the people who were there for them when they were growing up, and how they made an impact on the young people they know today.

Life Freaks Me Out and Then I Deal with It by K. L. Hong. This down-to-earth memoir touches on hard-hitting issues—drugs, alcohol, self-esteem, relationships, sex—to emphasize to today's teens the power of choice, and the importance of finding their own values and truths as they grow up. Author K. L. Hong takes readers on a candid journey of her own teen years (and the years since), offering young people guidance on answering life's big questions: Who am I? What's important to me? For any teenager who has ever thought, "Sometimes life DOES freak me out!" this book will be a warm confidant, a caring guide, and a compassionate friend.

Me@My Best: Ideas for Staying True to Yourself—Every Day. A tool designed specifically to introduce Developmental Assets to the very people who stand the most to benefit: youth! This booklet was inspired by the voices of many young people throughout North America who know assets and how to communicate the power of "keeping it real" to their peers. Speaking directly to young people, the booklet introduces the framework in a youth-friendly way, encourages them to explore what the categories mean to them personally, and inspires them to find and build upon their own strengths. *Me@My Best* includes: youth descriptions of the eight asset categories and what the categories mean to them; real stories from real young people; reflection questions to deepen a young person's understanding of the assets; and suggestions on how young people can make an impact when building assets for themselves and their peers.

More Than Just a Place to Go: How Developmental Assets Can Strengthen Your Youth Program (Video). Based on three different out-of-school programs in three different states and settings, this video shows how to intentionally create and foster a developmentally-attentive environment, staff, and program for young people. Inspirational and informative, this video offers firsthand accounts from program administrators, staff, volunteers, parents, community leaders, and youth participants as well. The video highlights specific asset-building programs, practices, and strategies that can be used to help motivate and strengthen any out-of-school program. Great tool for in-service and new staff trainings.

More Than Just a Place to Go: How Developmental Assets Can Strengthen Your Youth Program by Yvonne Pearson, Kristin Johnstad, and James Conway. The companion to the inspirational and informative *More Than Just a Place to Go* video, this book encourages youth programs to integrate assets into their current programs. It profiles and uses examples from a variety of successful, yet distinctly different, youth programs: a faith-based city after-school program for students in grades 8 through 12, a neighborhood multisite activity program focused on learning opportunities, and an after-school YMCA tutorial program for 6- to 15-year-olds.

Authored by veteran youth program professionals with years of experience in the field, the book includes: supporting research behind assets and their proven, positive youth impact; celebration of programs' strengths; examples of engaging staff and leadership in introducing and using assets; and ideas for becoming more intentional with asset building.

Parenting at the Speed of Teens: Positive Tips on Everyday Issues. *Parenting at the Speed of Teens* is a practical, easy-to-use guide that offers positive, commonsense strategies for dealing with both the everyday issues of parenting teenagers—junk food, the Internet, stress, jobs, friends—and other serious issues teens may encounter: depression, divorce, racism, substance abuse. It illustrates how the daily "little things" such as talking one-on-one, setting boundaries, offering guidance, and modeling positive behavior make a big difference in helping a teenager be successful during these challenging, exciting years of adolescence. The book is written around common parent issues, questions, and frustrations. Parents will relate to the real-life dilemmas addressed in chapters on Home and Family, School, Friends and Peers, Work, Image, and Special Issues. Parents will find comfort and reassurance in the assets-based parenting perspective and advice.

Tag, You're It! 50 Easy Ways to Connect with Young People by Kathleen Kimball-Baker. This motivating book offers commonsense ideas to connect and build assets with young people. Youth workers, parents, educators, businesspeople, congregation leaders, and anyone who cares about youth will love this book. The *Tag, You're It!* card deck and the *Tag, You're It!* posters are also specifically designed to spark conversations between youth and adults.

Take It to the Next Level: Making Your Life What You Want It to Be by K. L. Hong. Created just for teens and young adolescents, *Take It to the Next Level* helps young people focus on their successes, explore what they really want and how to get it, and celebrate their efforts and accomplishments. Filled with activities and journal topics, this booklet guides young people through the journey of adolescence from a Developmental Asset approach. A companion booklet to Search Institute's *Me@My Best,* an introductory booklet on Developmental Assets for teens, *Take It to the Next Level* offers young people a chance to take the assets deeper by offering opportunity for more self-exploration and action.

What Teens Need to Succeed: Proven, Practical Ways To Shape Your Own Future by Peter L. Benson, Judy Galbraith, and Pamela Espeland. This book describes the 40 Developmental Assets that all teens need to succeed, then gives hundreds of suggestions teens themselves can use to build their own assets at home, at school, in the community, in their congregation, with friends, and with youth organizations. *What Teens Need to Succeed* inspires and empowers teens to build their own assets. It introduces the concept of asset building, invites readers to identify the assets they need in their lives, and gives specific suggestions on how to build them. Assets in Action sections show how people across the nation are creating healthy communities using the asset-building model. *Published by Free Spirit Publishing.*

Who, Me? Surprisingly Doable Ways You Can Make a Difference for Kids. Use this desktop perpetual calendar for reminders, tips, and inspiration in your daily interactions with kids and teens. Here you'll find great, concrete asset-building ideas from dozens of the best Search Institute youth publications.

WHY Do They Act That Way? A Survival Guide to the Adolescent Brain for You and Your Teen by David Walsh, Ph.D., with Nat Bennett. Even smart kids do stupid things. It's a simple fact of life. No one makes it through the teenage years unscathed—not the teens and not their parents. But now there's expert help for both generations in this groundbreaking new guide for surviving the drama of adolescence. In *WHY Do They Act That Way?*, National Institute on Media and Family's president and award-winning psychologist Dr. David Walsh explains exactly what happens to the human brain on the path from childhood into adolescence and adulthood. Revealing the latest scientific findings in easy-to-understand terms, Dr. Walsh shows why moodiness, quickness to anger and to take risks, miscommunication, fatigue, territoriality, and other familiar teenage behavior problems are so common—all are linked to physical changes and growth in the adolescent brain. *Published by Free Press.*

About the Author
Kareem Moody is the program director at P.A.R.K. (Positive Atmosphere
Reaches Kids), a comprehensive faith-based after-school program
for students in grades 8 through 12 who are in danger of dropping out of
school. He lives in Little Rock, Arkansas, with his wife and two sons.

About Search Institute
Search Institute is an independent nonprofit organization whose
mission is to provide leadership, knowledge, and resources to promote
healthy children, youth, and communities. To accomplish this mission,
the institute generates and communicates new knowledge, and
brings together community, state, and national leaders. For a free
information packet, call 800-888-7828 or visit our Web site at
www.search-institute.org.